*REF.*

*JAIME MOYER*

# ref AXL FOX
# THE OTHER SIDE
# OF THE BARRICADE

**JAIME MOYER**

*JAIME MOYER*

AXL FOX The Other Side Of The Barricade
(c) 2024 by Jaime Moyer
All Rights Reserved

ISBN: 979-8-3302-5574-0
ISBN (eBook): 979-8-3302-6374-5

All people, locations, events, and situations are portrayed to the best of the authors memory. While all of the events described are based on the professional wrestling referee career of Axl Fox, some names have been reduced to a first name or nickname bases to protect the privacy of the individual involved. All gimmicks belong to the wrestler and or promotion they are with. All names of promotions belong to the owner of that promotion.

No parts of this book may be reproduced, stored in retrieval system, or transmitted by any means without the written permission of the author and publisher.

Cover Photography by Jaime Moyer

Published in the United States of America

## DEDICATION

**To my trainer *"Twisted Tate"* Tate Hammer:**
Thank you for believing in me when no one else did. Thank you for giving me the opportunity no one else would. But most importantly Thank you for taking a chance on me knowing full well my medical condition could have been a liability.

**To my mother Sharon Cataldi:**
Thank you for being without a doubt, hands down my number one fan. Thank you for supporting my decision to be a referee in professional wrestling and encouraging me every step of the way. Thank you for being front row at every show you could be at cheering me on the loudest even when everyone else might have been booing me.

**To all my fans:**
Thank you for your support. Thank you for always being behind me. Thank you for your cheers and even for your boos. Without you there truly is no show. You guys are the key factor to making any show possible.

*JAIME MOYER*

# REF AXL FOX

# CONTENTS

**Entrance** ……………………………………………………9

**Chapter 1:** *Indie Mark* …..…………………………….13
**Chapter 2:** *Liability* ……..……………………………. 21
**Chapter 3:** *Training* ……..……………………….. 25
**Chapter 4:** *In Ring Security* ………………………… 35
**Chapter 5:** *More Then Just Counting* …..………… 43
**Chapter 6:** *Refereeing* …..…………………………… 53
**Chapter 7:** *TNA* ……..………………………………… 65
**Chapter 8:** *The Highlight Reel* …..………………… 71
**Chapter 9:** *The Ref-olution* …..…………………… 79
**Chapter 10:** *Retirement* ……..…………………… 83
**Chapter 11:** *Memories To Last A Lifetime* …..……… 95
**Chapter 12:** *Going Off Script* ….....………………… 115
**Chapter 13:** *Life After Retirement* ………………… 123

**Ring The Bell** …..……………………………………… 133

**About The Author** ……..……………………………… 137
**Acknowledgments** ……..……………………………… 139
**Author Other Titles** ……..……………………………… 141

*JAIME MOYER*

REF AXL FOX

## ENTERANCE

    I grew up in a not so financially blessed home. My mother and father did their best to provide for me and my sister. We grew up with cable, but when the internet became popular my dad had given my sister and I the choice of having cable or the internet. Of course since all the "cool kids" as well as all of our friends had the internet at the time, we wanted it as well. So my dad called the cable company the next day and canceled our cable and got our house hooked up with internet. This meant we would go back to antenna TV where we only had access to about 4 channels, maybe 6 channels on a really nice day.

    I forget exactly what show it was before SmackDown was a thing that aired on regular television, Heat or Velocity. That was the first wrestling show I started watching. Then SmackDown became a thing and was available on UPN which later re-branded to The CW. SmackDown was the very first major wrestling show I watched on television when I was in the late stages of elementary school. I was so hooked on wrestling at that time that I even managed to persuade my mother to buy me a WWE binder every year starting in about the four or fifth grade. Now as I previously stated we weren't exactly a family of money so my mother made it very clear that if she got me a WWE binder that was my one "big" item for that school year.

My sister always chose name brand clothing as her "big" item for the school year as all the girls her age where wearing clothing from Aeropostel, H&M, Ambercrombie & Fitch, Pac Sun, etc. We couldn't afford to buy the Pay-Per-Views so every Monday as I was getting ready for school. My mom would look up the results of the Pay-Per-View from the previous day and tell me the results of each match, and read me the highlights so I could stay up in the know when it came to what had happened. I also frequented WWE.com during my turn using the family computer so I could stay in the know when it came to what happened on Monday Night Raw. It wasn't until I went to college in 2010 that I had access to cable again and was able to watch Monday Night Raw and other promotions such as TNA Impact. I was such a fan of professional wrestling that when I was a teenager I broke my first bone, … well two bones.

The neighbor kid and one of my friends at that time Craig came over to hang out. We decided to go into the back yard and wrestle as we both were fans of professional wrestling. Craig lifted me upside down with his head between my legs and my head positioned down by his legs. I recognized this position from wrestling, It was the set up for The Undertakers finisher The Tombstone Piledriver. I kicked Craig in the face in an attempt to escape and my kick rocked him so hard he dropped me on the back of my neck. I got up and my right arm felt like someone had filled it with rocks and I couldn't move it.

    I went inside to tell my mom and she took me to the hospital where I was told I had broken my shoulder blade as well as my collar bone. The doctor put me in a sling and sent me on my way. All my friends during this time of my life were fans of professional wrestling just like I was. I talk about my friend Josh in my book *"Fearless Over Failure"* which is available through most major online retailers. I also love video games, My first system was the Nintendo Gamecube. My first wrestling video game was Day Of Reckoning 2.

    In 2010, WWE made a blog style fan page for it's fans, It was called WWE Fan Nation. I took interest in a form called IFWA which was a fantasy wrestling promotion where you'd create a show with a roster of superstars in the wrestling industry be is past or present. I originally called my show Top Dog Wrestling or TDW for short and the weekly show was called, Doghouse and I posted it ever Thursday. I stuck with that for the first season of the IFWA and ended up placing second place not far behind the forms creator who won first place. The second season I knew I had to work harder if I wanted first place so I re-branded a bit, I changed the name of my show to, Insane Fighting Alliance or IFA for short, and I called my weekly show Knockout and posted it every Saturday. I made the more extreme match types in wrestling a regular part of my show and I ended up taking first place in the second season. Right before the third season began WWE decided to shut down the WWE Fan Nation website to focus more of it's attention on the WWE Network.

    After WWE Fan Nation shut down my new interest became creating unique Create A Wrestler or CAW's on the WWE video games. Deathstar and Midnight are the OG's of my CAW creations. Beast Man, Merica Man and Angelina AI are three of my more recent CAW creations within the WWE Games that everyone seems to love when I upload them to the Community Creations to be downloaded. Beast Man's story is he is a survivalist that got lost in the wild for so long that he has begun to become farrell as though he is half man, half wild animal. Merica Man's story is that he is simply an American Luchador who has pride for his country of the United States Of America. Angelina AI, her story is that she is an artificial intelligence bot looking to take over the industry, specifically women's wrestling. Creating A Wrestler with an interesting backstory that makes the Community wanting to download them for themselves is a very enjoyable way for me to feed my interest in playing video games as well as to let my creative juices shine.

## Chapter I

## Indiemark

I attended my very first show on the independent circuit as a fan in the summer of 2015. My friend Chandler who went by the name of, "The Caribbean Superstar" CJ Cruz had invited me to the same as he was on the card for that night to have a match. Tickets were about $15 for general admission or $20 for Front Row in advanced and $20 for general admission or $25 for Front Row at the door, if I remember correctly. Beings I was friends with Chandler and he was part of the show I was able to get tickets in advanced through him and beings Front Row was only $5 more then general admission, Of course I always got front row! I wouldn't recommend going to a live professional wrestling show if you want to believe that professional wrestling is real. I say this because I remember watching a wrestler jump off the top turnbuckle and perform a missile dropkick onto another wrestler standing in the ring and seeing his feet go over the guys shoulders not even connect with the guys face.

The guy standing in the ring fell backwards onto the mat. I was sitting there like, "What the heck, He didn't even hit you!" But I wasn't going to let that stop me from having a good time. I enjoyed the show so much that I eventually told my mom about it and managed to get her to come to the shows with me. Mostly so I didn't have to sit alone the entire show, But that's besides the point. Little did I know this would be something my mother and I would look forward to every month and bond over.

The promotion I first attended was called, Atomic Championship Wrestling, and was located at a local fire station about a mile and a half from where I was living at the time. What I didn't know about ACW was that aside from my friend Chandler being on the roster, a cousin of mine though marriage on my moms side of the family Dan was a referee and his mom and dad, as well as his brothers occasionally, attended the shows as well. Dan refereed under the name Dan Marks and would later step down from refereeing and assume a position as a manager by the name of "Coach" Dan Marks. I also later found out that I was also related through marriage on my moms side of the family to another wrestler in ACW who wrestled by the name of "The Death Dealer" Bobby Kruger. I also found out that I lived about a mile away from the promoter of ACW, Twisted Tate. So when I couldn't get tickets from Chandler I would get a hold of Tate for tickets in advanced to the shows.

## *REF AXL FOX*

As I began to get more and more comfortable attending the ACW shows, I began to become more vocal and engaged as a fan in the crowd. I would cheer louder then anyone for my favorite wrestlers and boo louder then anyone at the wrestlers I didn't like. I remember one show the sound guy who was the child of one of the wrestlers, Scotty Jefferies, was having trouble with the sound system. After a while I started chanting, "FIRE THE SOUND GUY!" The entire crowd began to chant with me after a while. The next show I didn't see him working the sound system and later I found out that he indeed got fired from working the sound system. Now I don't know for sure that it was because of me, But one definitely has to wonder if my getting the entire fire hall to chant with me, "FIRE THE SOUND GUY" over and over wasn't the icing on the cake as far as him being fired.

A few shows after the first ACW show I attended I was sitting in my seat, front row of course, and one of the female managers by the name of Rabid Rizzo was laying out her promo pictures on the side of the ring for people to purchase. She saw me and walked up to me asking if I was enjoying the show. I told her I was and then she told me I should buy one of her promo pictures and that she would even autograph it for me. I agreed and gave her the money for a promo picture and she told me to pick one out that I liked. I picked one of her promo pictures from a modeling session she had obviously done and she autographed it and handed it to me. Little did she know, She created a monster in me that fed on collecting professional wrestling pictures and autographs as every show after that I walked away with at least one persons promo picture and autograph.

By this time I had pretty much become a regular at the Atomic Championship Wrestling shows. Everyone know me, if not by name then as "that loud mouth that always sits front row." I'm pretty sure I even made some of the people sitting around me uncomfortable with all my hooting and hollering as it would most of the time draw attention by the wrestlers and managers in the ring. I even at one point began to make signs and bring them to the shows. Chandler even after a while asked me to design some promo pictures for him so that he could sell them at the shows. Beings I attended college for Graphic Design I took on the task and hooked him up.

I use to pick on Chandler all the time telling him he was the John Cena of ACW because he didn't do very many moves outside of his normal set of moves. The favorite thing for the wrestlers and manager to do to me was to take my hat and toss it clean across the fire hall so I'd have to get up and go get it. I always wore a hat during this period of my life and I absolutely HATED when anyone would touch my hat. Beings I know if I touched any of the wrestlers or managers as a fan I would be asked to leave and never be able to come to an ACW show again per ACW policy on fans who get kicked out of a show. Bobby was a big one for taking my hat and whipping it across the fire hall. Nobody was off limits from heckling.

## *REF AXL FOX*

I remember at one show, there was this female wrestler by the name of Kaitlin Diemond who would come out with a bottle of "sake." I say "sake" because it was obviously water as no person in their right mind would be drinking a bottle of sake before their match. I also know it was water because I forget what exactly I said to her, but I think it was something along the lines of, "You Suck!" She took a big swig of the "sake" and spit it right in my face. As she walked away I yelled, "Spitters Are Quitters!" She kept walking around the ring and then eventually got into the ring where I continued to boo her and heckle her some more.

At another one of the shows Bobby had a match where he got tossed to the outside of the ring and he landed HARD. And when I say he landed hard, I mean I heard his head CRACK off the concrete floor. I said to him, "Are you OK?" and of course since he was a heel he told me to "Shut Up!" I said, "No, Seriously Bobby you're bleeding!" When he realized he was bleeding, and not just a little, he got back in the ring and him and his opponent ended the match shortly there after so Bobby could go get medical attention.

My favorite memory as a fan from attending the ACW shows though isn't even something I said or did. It comes from a show where the big name superstar that was to be in attendance was none other then Steve Corino. Steve was part of a tag team match and was positioned on the ring apron waiting to be tug in by his partner. This little kid next to me kept yelling, "Steve, Steve, Hey Steve, Steve!" Clearly annoyed with the kid, Steve turned around and said, "What do you want, Can't you see I'm working here?!" The kid yelled, "You're a B***H", Now there was no way this kid was more then like 12 years old MAYBE.

One show a wrestler by the name of Rob Noxious was fighting his opponent on the outside of the ring. I had just went to the concession stand and got 2 cheeseburgers as I was feeling kind of hungry. I was eating the one cheeseburger and then Rob reached over the barricade grabbed the other cheeseburger and shoved it in his opponents mouth. I was thinking to myself, "Hey, I was gonna eat that!" But I'd be lying if I didn't say it was pretty fun and in all fairness Rob did come up to me after and offer to buy me another cheeseburger, I told him it was alright and that he didn't have to do that.

Sabu from ECW was the featured Superstar of one of the ACW shows I attended before ACW had barricades. I was as always sitting front row and Sabu sat up a table right in front of me, He put his opponent on the table and his manager began yelling something to me. I couldn't understand him with his heavy Arabic accent but once I saw Sabu hit the ropes on the far side of the ring, I knew EXACTLY what his manager was saying to me. He was telling me to get out of the way, As Sabu dove through the ropes and onto the table I had moved out of the way in time but nearly got kicked in the head by Sabu. The table didn't break though, which was kind of disappointing.

## *REF AXL FOX*

From what I heard Sabu was quite upset about that and even raised some heck backstage about it.

    Another show the big name superstar to be in attendance was Robbie E from TNA Impact. During intermission I went back to the merchandise area and Robbie was at his merch table. I was the second person in line, the guy in front of me got something and handed Robbie a twenty dollar bill. Robbie said, "Oh, Do you got anything smaller, I don't really got change right now." They guy said that he didn't have anything smaller so I offered to give him change. Robbie thanked me and then when it was my turn to get merchandise he said to me, "I'll tell you what, I'll give you your change from helping that other guy or I'll cut you a deal on two promo pictures for the price of one, and I'll even autograph them both." I told Robbie I was only really interested in one picture so when he got enough change to pay me back, he did.

    So I tell people for about thirty seconds of my life, TNA Superstar Robbie E owed me $20. Eventually a few fellow fans at the ACW shows began to ask me jokingly, "When are you going to get into the ring?" I always laughed at the joke but eventually it began to become a serious thought in my mind. "Why don't I become a wrestler, I love wrestling, and it can't be that hard." Knowing I have a seizure disorder I thought it would be best to consult my neurologist about it. Needless to say, My neurologist wasn't a fan of the idea and shot it down real quickly.

## *JAIME MOYER*

He told me that being a wrestler was out of the question along with other things like operating a vehicle that requires a CDL license such as trucking or being a bus driver, etc. He said, "All it would take is one go hit to the head and you could go into a seizure." Obviously I was disappointed, but on the same hand I completely understood where he was coming from. So I evicted the thought of ever become a wrestler from my mind and moved on with life as a fan. Until one day I had a genius idea, "My neurologist said I couldn't be a Wrestler or a Manger, He said nothing about being a Referee." Also I wondered, "Do I really gotta tell him if I do become a referee?"

## CHAPTER II

## LIABILITY

    I began to try and find a wrestling school near me to begin training at. Now at this point in time I knew that Tate own atomic Championship Wrestling but I was unaware that he also did wrestling training at his house. I knew that Rob Noxious was the owner of CCW and had a wrestling school called Fort Noxious Wrestling Academy, which if I'm correct was based out of Lebanon, PA at the time, So I hit him up for training. He messaged me back and said something along the lines of, "That's a bit far for you to travel just to train isn't it, Why don't you try talking to Tate?" Now aside from not knowing Tate did training as well, I didn't really want to work for ACW because by this time Chandler has left ACW and was working at another promotion. I did tell Rob that I do have a seizure disorder and that the doctor wouldn't let me wrestle so that's why I wanted to be a referee, So I figure Rob also might have told me what he told me to avoid admitting he didn't want to take the risk of me being a liability to Classic Championship Wrestling aka CCW.

Chandler at this time was working for Regional Championship Wrestling, aka RCW, which was in Reading, PA. I messaged the owner of that promotion as well, Ray Torres, and well he pretty much told me the same thing Rob Noxious had told me. Again I'm pretty sure that was his way of giving me the nice version of "Your seizure disorder could pose a liability to RCW and that not a risk I'm willing to take. There was also the Wild Samoans training school in Allentown, PA which sure that would have been cool to be trained by the Wild Samoans of WWE but I also knew I couldn't afford their school. Eventually I swallowed my pride and I messaged Tate. I also informed Tate about my seizure disorder.

Tate had told me that he would train me and saw the fact that I have a seizure disorder as an opportunity to put that he trained someone with a health risk to his resume. I didn't think that finding a place to train would take such effort. Part of me was glad though that out of everyone I messaged Tate was the one willing to train me. I trusted Tate which is a major key in being trained for professional wrestling. I was so excited to start training, I had ordered a pair of AMA high impact knee pads as Tate said that is what most of the guys in the big leagues like WWE wear. Tate had also given me a referee shirt that was a size to big for me, but I made it work.

## *REF AXL FOX*

I also had a lot of respect for Tate as about a year after I started attending ACW shows I was involved in a really bad car wreck on the way home from a RCW show. I had multiple internal injuries and spent a week in the ICU of the hospital. The week I spent in the ICU of the hospital also happened to be the week of the next ACW show and I had already had my ticket. I messaged Tate and told him what had happened and that I wouldn't be able to make the show. Tate messaged me back and told me not to worry and that he would honor my ticket for that show at the next months show. When it came time for the next months show I went to the show and Tate was a man of his word. He indeed honored my ticket form the previous months show.

I started training in November of 2018 which happened to be just a month after I began to self harm. I promised myself I'd never take my own life or purposefully harm myself in any way, no matter how bad things got in my life. And I broke that promise to myself which filled me with shame, regret, guilt, and so many more negative emotions. I knew that there are a ton of men and women in professional wrestling that will tell you that wrestling "saved their life." So I saw this training for professional wrestling thing as a way to distract my mind from my problems and hopefully take my mind off of the urge to self harm. And to a point I wasn't wrong because it did help me control my self harming.

My next struggle I had to worry about now that I had a trainer and was hooked up with a place to train was that at 6ft 3in and 130 lbs I was technically underweight. Heck, A cruiserweight could crush me. I weighed as much as most female wrestlers in the big leagues. So I got myself hooked up to a gym membership and told myself I was going to start eating healthier. That didn't last long as after going to the gym and seeing no results and nothing I liked to eat being healthy to eat, I gave up all that real fast. My high metabolism that I inherited from my fathers genetics cursed me to being a twig for all eternity.

## CHAPTER III

## TRAINING

Now before I get to my training with Tate, I did have a little bit of professional wrestling training prior to my training with Tate. In I think it was 2016 Chandler wanted to try and start his own professional wrestling promotion. He reached out to me to see if I was interested and told me his friend BJ, Brian, and Brian's brother Chris were all on board with the idea. I told Chandler that would be awesome and that I could be the referee. We were going to make this promotion more of a backyard wrestling promotion. So we started getting together and Chandler started to show us some basic professional wrestling moves.

My plan was to not only be a referee but to change the game as to what a professional wrestling referee was. I pitched the idea to Chandler and he loved it. I told

## *JAIME MOYER*

Chandler I wanted to have entrance music and I didn't want to wear the typical black and white stripped shirt, I wanted something different. I even started crafting an idea for a gimmick as a referee. I was going to be known as "The Ref-olution" a mix between your standard referee and what you don't expect from a standard referee. I wanted my entrance music to be "Edge Of A Revolution" by Nickleback.

My plan for being a professional wrestling referee in Chandler's promotion was to start a revolution when it came to being a referee in professional wrestling. I was going to take the standard of being a referee and completely throw it out the window and take it to a whole new level. We met a few times for training and then for some reason or another we ended up not continuing to train and then eventually the idea of starting a promotion together died out. I don't even know if anyone even really noticed because no one really said anything regarding it. But this was the first time I'd ever train for professional wrestling. Now fast forward a few years later to then end of 2018.

I began training with Tate in November of 2018. Since it was winter and freezing cold out we trained inside the basement of the barn Tate had. He had old amateur wrestling mats from the high school near by laid on the floor. The mats were only a inch or two thick so they didn't provide much cushioning especially since the cold made them stiff as a board. Tate had us all get in a circle and we began to stretch. Tate stressed the importance of stretching and making sure you're loosened up before getting down to business.

    I'd be lying if I said I wasn't at least a little bummed out that we weren't training in the ring but on the other hand I was glad we were training somewhere where it was at least somewhat warm. After we were all stretched out and loosened up it was time for squats. I don't think I ever did a single squat in my life prior to this day. Tate told us that he wanted us to do 250 squats. I was thinking to myself, "You're crazy, Ain't no way I'm doing 250 squats!" Honestly though, At about 70 squats I felt like my legs were going to give out on me and my bowels were gonna unload everywhere.

    As I continued to push through the pain and tried my hardest to maintain good posture my legs began more and more to feel like jelly. That two hundred and fiftieth squat hurt so bad but mentally it was so good as I knew we were done. Tate told us that we better get comfortable doing that many squats because his goal was to get us to a point we could do 500 squats. We all looked at him like, "You're off your rocker, Tate!" He then informed us that in big promotions like Ring Of Honor they are expected to do a thousand squats and in promotions like WWE their expected to do even more then a thousand squats. Thankfully, unlike every other person who comes to the indies, I had no desire to take my career out of the indies and into the big leagues.

## *JAIME MOYER*

Little did I know that a few short weeks later we would accomplish that goal of doing 500 squats and it felt so good. We all were so proud of ourselves, We truly earned this great accomplishment and fed of the momentum of it. Tate even took a group picture of us and posted it on social media and officially welcomed us to "The 500 Squat Club!" After stretching, strengthening, and conditioning we would move on to learning how to take a bump. I was especially excited for this because this is what I signed up for baby! We were finally getting down to what we all were here for, learning how to become a professional wrestler.

Or in my case to become a professional wrestling referee. I remember taking my first bump, I believe we started with front bumps. My turn came to take my first front bump and it was obvious that I was scared and that I didn't know what I was doing. I was absolutely terrible and it showed. Plus when I hit the cold hard mat and felt how unforgiving it was, That didn't help my confidence either. I had a lot to learn if I wanted to make it out of training.

All I knew though was I wasn't going to be one of those guys who give up in training and go home and never come back. Next we moved on to back bumps and surprise to surprise, I was no better at back bumps then I was a front bumps. Tate even at one point said to me, "Jaime, You're smacking the back of your head on the mat, That's a good way to give yourself a concussion!" I was trying so incredibly hard to do my best and do the bumps right. Tate could eventually see I was honestly trying my best and he said to me, "Don't overthink it, Just do it." He was right though, I was overthinking things.

Every time it was my turn a million things would run through my mind. Things like, "OK, Were gonna do this right this time" or "This time we aren't gonna screw up." Each time I wouldn't do things right I would become very frustrated with myself as I don't take failure very well. All I could do though was to try even hard until I got things down. Night after night, I would go home from training and if I wasn't sore after training, I was definitely sore by the next morning. But I refused to give up!

After our training sessions, especially during the winter months, Tate would invite us to come into his house after training to warm up before we went home. We'd normally all gather in the living room and talk with each other. Sometimes we'd have one big conversation, other times there would be half a dozen conversations if not more going on at once. This was also often the time that in the kitchen Tate would collect our training dues for the month or whatever. After a while we would all leave and head home. We usually trained Monday through Friday 7pm-8pm, sometimes later.

Once winter was over and the warmer months would hit, training looked a bit different. We would start training by setting up the ring in Tate's yard. After the ring was set up we'd get into the ring. This was the first time that I ever stood inside of a professional wrestling ring. It felt so good to stand in that ring. I just wanted to run back and forth from rope to rope, turnbuckle to turnbuckle, and jump as high as I could off the top turnbuckle and come crashing down to the mat below. But I knew I had to contain my excitement and stay professional and focused on the true task at hand, training.

Now that we could train in the ring, We could do a lot more then we could on the cold, hard amateur wrestling mats in Tate's basement of the barn. We did our front bumps and back bumps, which I was still pretty terrible at and raised concern by anyone watching me do them. But we also learned how to move around the ring and roll around the ring. I absolutely loved doing the rolling drills, they were my favorite. We'd get in the ring most times in groups of four, we would take a corner each. Tate would say, "1..2..3...roll" and we would front roll from corner to corner until we ended up back at the corner we started in. Then the next set of people would come in the ring and do the same thing. Next would be back rolls, They were pretty basic. We would assume a seating position, fall backwards, and roll over onto our head and back onto our feet.

After we got all that down, We would learn how to run the ropes. I was also excited for this as on television they guys looked so cool running the ropes. I remember the first time I hit the ropes, I was like, "Dang, That kinda hurts!" I'm pretty sure a few times I left training with an imprint of the ropes or worse rope burn on my side. But again, I wasn't going to let a little rope burn or marks stop me from giving my all. Again giving up was not an option!

After I got all that down Tate started to have me focus a little less on the wrestlers drills and started to introduce me to referee things such as my positioning in the ring, ring awareness, counting, interaction with the wrestlers in the ring, etc. Honestly, I never did really find this to be much fan as what the wrestlers were doing looked ten times more fun then what I was doing. But Tate was the trainer and I was the trainee so I didn't complain. I did exactly what I was told to do. Training ended up not being all sunshine and rainbows though. Our jogging around Tate's parking lot would eventually bring a personal issue of mine to light.

One day when we were doing our typical job around the parking lot, I noticed I was getting really out of breath and my heart was pounding. I went up to Tate and told him how I was feeling. He told me, "Don't give up brother, Push through it, You got this!" I continued to push through the pain and breath the best I could but it only got worse and worse. Eventually I could hear my breaths deep down in my lungs and they sounded really shallow and rapid. I went up to Tate again and said, "I don't know man, Something really isn't right."

He told me to take seat and rest for a bit and see how I feel. Eventually my breathing went back to normal and my heart stopped pounding. I ultimately decided after training to go to the doctor and get things checked out.

## *JAIME MOYER*

Luckily I did because after running some tests and doing some imagery on my chest it was discovered that I have a tutiptic heart valve which is simpler terms, a leaky heart valve. My one heart valve doesn't completely close all the way when I breath. This was the result of injuries I had sustained in my near fatal car crash in 2016 haunting me.

Tate would occasionally have "special guests" come to our training sessions to offer us some of their knowledge. One time Tate had Teddy Hart show us a thing or two. Eventually Tate would get into a relationship and later marry legendary female wrestling icon LuFisto and he had her shed some of her knowledge upon us a time or two in training. It wasn't always big name superstars though, Sometimes he'd have veterans of ACW like Dame Smith or even Rockin' Rebel teach us a thing or two. Though to be fair Rockin' Rebel did compete in WWF until the mid 90's. Later in my training Tate would have one of the referee's of ACW by the name of Larry Peace take me under his wing and mentor me a bit so to say.

As I trained with Tate and some of the other wrestlers from the ACW roster who would attend the training sessions as well, I continued to attend the ACW shows as a fan and sit in the crowd. But training did have it's benefits when it came to being a fan at the shows. I would show up to the shows early to help set up for the show and I would stay late to help tear down the ring and the set from the show. This meant also before the show, before they'd let people into the fire hall I'd get to sit backstage with the wrestlers, managers, referees, etc. This was the first time I'd ever been backstage at a wrestling show. Helping to set up for the show had it's benefits as well as It meant I got to pick where my seat would be for the show.

Times would eventually get tough for me financially and I told Tate that I couldn't afford to pay for training anymore. He told me not to worry about it and that he wanted me to continue to come to training regardless. He told me I could pay him what I could, when I could. February of 2019 Tate would call me into his office upstairs in his house. LuFisto was up there as well on the computer and when I got into his office, Tate handed me a contract for an official referee position with Atomic Championship Wrestling. He told me it was a standard contract with the addition that if anybody maliciously hits me in my head or does anything that causes me to have a seizure they will not only be reprimanded but held responsible for my medical bills.

This was a moment that really increased the amount of respect I have for Tate. Though, I knew full well none of the people at ACW would ever maliciously intend to make me have a seizure. They all seemed like nice people outside of the ring regardless of their gimmick in the ring. Tate and LuFisto both explained to me the responsibility of signing my contract and the expectations that come with signing my contract. Tate told me to look it over, get familiar with the details of it and then when I was ready to sign on the dotted line. To be honest I never

## *JAIME MOYER*

skimmed a document so fast in my life and signed on the line, making me an OFFICAL referee of Atomic Championship Wrestling!

# CHAPTER IV

## IN RING SECURITY

During this time in my life my mental health had gotten absolutely out of control. I began to self harm in October of 2018 just one month before I began my professional wrestling training. By March of 2019 I had fifteen anxiety attacks in the span of about four and a half months. I had self harmed numerous times throughout those four and a half months. I knew now that I was under contract with ACW that I was expected to be a positive influence within the company and that meant being an example for the fans. I most certainly didn't want people to see me self harming and think that was something I encouraged or supported.

I made the decision to get help for not only my self harming but for my mental health as well. The local hospital in my area evaluated me and determined that I didn't need to be admitted to the Inpatient Program. I definitely needed help so they discharged me and referred me to an Intensive Outpatient Program instead. I go more in depth about this in my book, *"Fearless Over Failure."* I spent the next 5 months in the Intensive Outpatient Program before my therapist would contact the hospital and request for me to be discharged from the program. Getting help for my mental health was one of the greatest decisions I've ever made in my life.

After I signed my contract with ACW and was officially part of the roster, Tate had informed me that I wasn't ready just yet to be a referee but that I was no longer a fan either. He told me, "I want you to start paying attention to the referee's during the show and really study them in the ring. So for that reason I want you sitting in a corner ringside so you can get an up close and personal view of the action in the ring while working In Ring Security." I was super excited to say the least, I had never been on the side of the barricade where the action happens as I knew as fan in the crowd that was grounds for getting kicked out and barred from any future shows ever. March of 2019 would be my first official show that I was a part of the ACW roster for. Normally ACW shows where held at the Stevens Fire Company but this particular show we were traveling to Allentown, Pennsylvania to Game Changer World to do a show there.

I had absolutely no idea where in the head this place was so I asked Tate if I could get a ride with somebody to the venue. He told me I could ride in the equipment truck with Scotty Jefferies. I got in the truck put my seat belt on and waited for Scotty nervously. I was nervous cause I knew Scotty as a fan of him, I never really talked to him before and now I had to ride in a uHaul with him for the next 2 hours give or take. Scotty opened the driver side door of the uHaul and climbed in. I feel like he could sense I was nervous so to crack the ice he said, "You smoke?"

    I said, "No, I don't" he said, "Yeah, Ya do, You look like an old head!" I had no idea what he meant by an "old head" but again I said, "No, I don't smoke." He said, "Alright well do you mind if I smoke?" I told him that I didn't mind and went back to being silent and nervous. Scotty continued to talk to me on the drive to the venue. I could tell he was genuinely making an effort to get to know me.

    We arrived at the venue and Scotty got out to ask Tate where he should park the uHaul. After Scotty got parked we got out and everyone went into the Game Changer World venue to see what we were working with for the show. We then began to set up the ring, the lighting, the stage area, and even the seating for the fans. Once we got everything set up I took a chair and found the corner of the ringside area with the most space so I wouldn't be in the way during the show and sat my chair in the corner. Every minute closer to show time that passed my excitement grew more and more out of control. When it came time for the show, the roster went backstage and Tate told me to help Dawn aka "Wrestling Mom" and

## *JAIME MOYER*

Scotties wife at the time at the door with making sure everyone had entrance bracelets upon paying for their ticket so we know they paid to get in. Of course I did as I was told.

    This night I would also learn a very valuable lesson in being a part of the show, but I would learn it the hard way. Once showtime came, I went to my seat in the corner of the ringside area and Tate had told me it was not only my job to keep the fans behind the barricade but to take the wrestlers clothing and accessories and what not used for their entrance to the back and to hold on to any any all championship belts being defended in the match. It was time for Scotty to have his match, Knowing he was a bad guy as he came out to the ring I began to boo him. He made his way around the ring and when he got to me he slapped me damn near right out of my chair and to the floor. This wasn't a fake slap, This was an actual full force slap. I sat back up in my chair kinda laughing a bit as I had just seen my first bit of action in my time on the ACW roster.

    During intermission I went backstage and one of the guys I trained with who wrestles under the name Jack Hershey said to me, "You don't heckle the talent!" I knew he was right and that he had a point so the rest of the night I refrained from heckling anyone else on the roster. After the show on the way home, Scotty explained to me why he slapped me the way he did and told me that some guys aren't so nice when it comes to stuff like that. Scotty Jefferies was a veteran of ACW and of course I had a lot of respect for him so I apologized to him and told him it wouldn't happen again. From this point on I told myself, "We need to work on turning fan mode off and work mode on when it comes to showtime." But other then that, I had officially survived my very first show under contract with Atomic Championship Wrestling.

During my time working In Ring Security I would get to be part of my first ten bell salute. A ten bell salute is a way a promotion pays respect to the passing of one of their talents, staff, loyal fans, etc. My first ten bell salute would be in memory of the passing of a man I had much respect for as a fan but didn't get to really know during my time under contract with ACW as he took his life about two and a half months after I began working ACW shows as In Ring Security. Rockin' Rebel had taken the life of his wife and then taken his own life in June of 2018. Rockin' Rebel was one of the people who told me I should get involved in professional wrestling so that was where the foundation of my respect for him stemmed from. A ten bell salute usually happens at the start of the show and everyone backstage surrounds the ring, and everyone in the crowd stands at their seats as whoever is in charge of the ring bell dings the bell ten times slowly.

I stood at my chair in the corner as the person manning the ring bell rang the bell, ding, … ding, … ding, … ding, … ding …, ding, … ding, … ding, … ding, … ding! I could feel the emotions of sadness and grief that flooded through the venue as not only I had much respect for Rebel but everyone respected the absolute heck out of

## JAIME MOYER

Rockin' Rebel. At the conclusion of a ten bell salute, generally everyone claps and everyone around the ring pounds as hard as they can on the ring mat. Then everyone around the ring goes to the back, the crowd takes their seats and the show begins. Rockin' Rebel was a true inspiration to me and I'm thankful for everything he taught me in the short time we did work under ACW together. That wouldn't be the last ten bell salute I'd be a part of but it sure as heck was one of the ones that impacted me the most.

I worked In Ring Security for the next 4 months and rarely ever did I encounter any problems. I only ever really had to ask a fan to keep her young daughter from crawling in and out of the barricade sections maybe once. Aside from that, It seemed like when the wrestlers brought things to the outside, that they enjoyed seeing if they could throw their opponent into where I was sitting and squash me like a bug. I remember one time the women where in action and came to the outside and the one tossed her opponent towards where I was sitting and I just couldn't get out of the way fast enough and her opponent landed right in my lap. Words can't describe how awkward and embarrassed I felt. Also during this time I would get to feel just how heavy a real wrestling championship belt was as on numerous occasions I was responsible for keeping the title belts safe while the match took place.

I remember one show, I forget who it was exactly but they were a bad guy. They came up to me and demanded I give them the title belt. The match wasn't over and no one told me this was part of the match so I wasn't sure what to do. All I knew was I wasn't about to argue with anyone, nor did I want to disrespect anyone. I handed the wrestler the title belt and they took it into the ring to use it as a weapon. It was kind of nice to see the wrestlers and managers giving me a little spotlight during their matches from time to time, and it really helped me warm up to being on the side of the barricade where the action takes place.

***JAIME MOYER***

## CHAPTER V

## MORE THEN JUST COUNTING

The thing about the indies is that generally there is no ring crew, stage crew, etc that is responsible for setting up and tearing down before and after the shows like there is in the big leagues. Most promotions on the indies rely on everyone involved in the show to lend a hand in helping prepare for the show. Heck sometimes Tate even left loyal, dedicated fans who were regulars at the shows aid in setting up and tearing down the shows. It really is one of those things where the more hands you got on deck, the faster it will get done. Tate made it very clear among the talent and workers at ACW that EVERYONE was expected to help before and after the shows. I'll talk more about this in another chapter.

Training the week of a show was a bit different then any other week. The closer we got to the day of the show the more we'd focus less on drills and more on what was going to take place at the shows. Monday to

Thursday we would training like normal, then on Friday we would train a little like normal but then we would focus on loading up the uHaul with the ring, barricades, stage equipment, etc We never trained on the weekends but Saturday was the day we had our shows. No one was allowed to leave training on Friday, without permission from Tate himself, until the uHaul was all packed up and the back door of the uHaul was latched and locked. Only then were we allowed to leave.

    Honestly, I dreaded having to load up the truck before a show because the thing about training was that there was most of the time only like six to eight people there so it took a good hour and a half to two hours to load up the truck. Once we got to the venue there would be more hands on deck to help set up so it only took about an hour or hour and a half to set up for the show itself. I feel like there always seemed to be less people who came to training the day before a show then there was at training a day there was no show the next day. But again that's an issue we will talk about in another chapter. Trust me that chapter is going to be a good one as I have quite a few things to unload about. Definitely gonna expose a few things that nobody talks about regarding the industry.

    Once the uHaul was packed and it was the day of the show, we would head to the venue of the show. Once we got to the venue of the show and the uHaul was parked, we would begin unloading the equipment and begin setting up for the show. Again, EVERYONE was expected to help set up for the show. Usually we would break up into two focus groups. One group would focus on putting the ring and ringside area together and the other group would focus on setting up the stage area. Once those two things were together we would start setting up the chairs for the crowd.

Before one of our shows we had at the Reverb I had been helping to set up the ring prior to the show. Now Tate made it very clear that wearing jeans to wrestle in was not ideal as far as wrestling attire due to jeans restricting your mobility. So of course I never wore jeans when I refereed but going to and from the shows I would often wear jeans. Well this particular show while we were setting up for it, I decided to take a short cut to the backstage area and instead of going through the curtain I decided to go up on the stage at the venue and go to the backstage area that way. I hiked my right leg up onto the stage as that is my dominate leg and I head the sound of ripping. I immediately know I had just ripped my pants!

I looked to the back of my pants to find them completely in tact. The inside of my right leg felt unusually airy then normal. I had looked at the right leg of my pants to find a rip from the inside of my knee all the way up to the crotch of my pants. Completely embarrassed I tried to think of a solution. Now at this particular show Facade and Dani Mo where scheduled to be part of the show so I knew Facade sold bandannas as part of his merchandise. I immediately went in search of Facade to obtain a bandanna to hid the gaping hole in my jeans. I couldn't find Facade but I found Dani Mo.

## *JAIME MOYER*

I had told Dani what happened and asked her if I could get a bandanna from Facades merchandise, I told her I would even pay for it. She dug out the bandannas from Facades merchandise bag and asked me what color I wanted. I told her I didn't care what color it was, and she told me to pick a color. I told her, "OK, Just give me a red one." She handed me a red bandanna and I handed her ten dollars. I then took the bandanna and wrapped it around my leg to hopefully keep the hole in my jeans shut.

Now the thing about this situation is that, Now I'm in downtown Reading, Pennsylvania with a red bandanna wrapped around my leg. Anyone with half a brain knows Gangs frequent the cities, red is synonymous with the Bloods, and Gangsters and Thugs tend to wear bandannas with the color of their gang around places like their wrists, their head, or THEIR LEG! It was maybe one o'clock in the afternoon at this point and the show was only scheduled to take place at seven o'clock in the afternoon meaning we had tons of time to roam the city or do whatever we wanted. Now mind you we are also only a block or two from where the "ladies of the night" frequent in Reading. I also knew we would eventually leave the venue to go to a nearby restaurant for some grub before the show. Now I had to venture through the downtown area with red bandanna wrapped around my leg, But thankfully I ended up having no problems.

After everything was set up and ready to go for the show, we were free to do whatever we wanted until about an hour or two prior to the doors opening for the show.

## *REF AXL FOX*

Some of the people would stay at the venue and talk and joke around, while others would go to a nearby restaurant and grab what most of the times would be some lunch. I enjoyed being part of the group of people that would go grab some lunch. When we ran a show at the Stevens Fire Hall we most of the time went to a nearby Sushi restaurant that we all enjoyed and frequented quite often, especially the day of a show. When we ran a show at the Reverb in Reading we usually went about a block or two away from the Reverb to a nice little sports bar and grill called, The Pike Cafe. One time when we went to The Pike Cafe I noticed they served Wild Bore Burgers and I just had to try it, It wasn't half bad if I'm being honest!

Usually if we weren't back at the venue by five o'clock we knew we want to be thinking about getting back to the venue as doors would open at six o'clock. Once we got back to the venue it was time to thing about getting into our gear for the show. I never liked getting dressed or undressed in a locker room setting. It was one of the biggest things I hated about school and about gym class. Instead of changing with everyone else in the locker room for the show I would go to the rest room of the venue and would change in one of the bathroom stalls instead. No one ever questioned me or said anything about this but I was fine with that as it was a personal choice and not like I was excommunicated from the locker room itself.

Now the thing about when I would get dressed for a show was I always tucked in my referee shirt into my pants and I always wore a belt regardless of weather my pants fit or not. It bugs the absolute crap out of me when you watch wrestling on television or play a wrestling video game, etc and the referee has their shirt untucked and it's hanging down over their pants. It's just such a messy look to me for someone who is supposed to be an authority figure in the ring and commands respect in the ring. So for that reason I always tucked my shirt into my pants. Once I was dressed and ready to go for the show I would head back to the backstage area and if the women were done changing and everyone was able to go back into the locker room area I would and I'd talk and joke around with the others. At this time we would also look at the card for the show and the wrestlers would talk to whoever was involved in their match about what they wanted to do in their match and how they wanted to do it, etc

At this time I would go to everyone I was assigned to their match and I would let them know that I was going to be the referee for their match. I'd also ask them if their was any major spots I should know about and what the finish of their match was going to look like. It was important that I knew the finish of the match so that I know what to look for signifying when to and how to end the match. Also talking to the wrestlers about how the match would go also gave me clarity when it came to if anything happened in the match that wasn't planned such as a legit injury or something along those lines. It was not only my job to be the authority in the ring but to also make sure no one got seriously injured during the match and if they did, getting the proper help to the ring in the right amount of time to keep the injury the least serious as possible while giving the fans the match they came to see. Most referees every carry black medical gloves in their pockets during a match just in case any blood or other bodily fluids would happen to make themselves present during the match.

    I remember my first match where blood became present. It was in 2019 during a one on one match between Ashley America and I don't remember who her opponent was. I noticed Ashley's lip was busted open and I asked her if she was alright. She told me that she was fine and I continue refereeing the match like so. There really is so much more that goes into refereeing then just counting to three or to ten. Just like wrestlers count on their opponent to be safe in the ring and keep them safe in the ring, the wrestlers also count on the referee to keep the match safe and all participants in the match safe.

    Once the door opened, which usually was at six o'clock to let the fans in, As a worker you stayed in the back. Unless you were going to be at your merchandise table selling merchandise prior to the start of the show, You left the backstage area for no reason outside going to the bathroom. If you talked to one fan, twenty more were gonna want to talk and next thing you know it's time to start the show and you're nowhere to be found holding up the start of the show. The show would begin when the venue lights would dim, the stage lights would take over and the sound of the shows intro music, in ACW's case was "The Stage" by Avenged Sevenfold, mixed with the roar of excitement from the crowd filled the venue. We usually had an area in the venue where workers could stand and watch the show without being noticed by the fans or being noticed by as few fans as possible. You didn't want fans taking notice of you and not focusing on what was going on in the ring as that could pose some heat backstage after the match by whoever was involved in the match as you taking their spotlight.

  During intermission of the show since I didn't sell merchandise, I would go out into the merchandise area and into the areas of the venue where the fans would be and I would talk with an associate with fans. A few times I did have fans ask to take pictures with me or if they could have my autograph in which I was always more then happy to give an opportunity like that to my fans. I'd also take this time to do a little marking out myself and get my picture taken and autograph with whoever the featured superstar was for that particular show if I couldn't catch them backstage. I always tried to make time for my fans as every good person in the industry of entertainment knows that you are nothing without your fans, and that without fans you have no job. The fans are literally what make the show, without fans your just two or more people rough housing like a bunch of elementary kids. I vowed to never be one of those people in the industry that was "too good for the fans."

  After the show was over and the fans began to clear out of the venue, It was time for everyone to, like expected, tear down the set much. Again we would do this usually in two focus groups. Just like setting up, one group would focus on tearing down the ring and ringside area and the other group would focus on tearing down the stage area. After that we'd clear out the chairs, put them away, and then we would sweep the venue floor of any garbage laying around. We'd load everything into the uHaul and once that was all loaded we were able to leave the venue. You would think now we got to go home and rest, but that's where you're wrong!

    We were expected to go from the venue back to Tate's house to help unload the uHaul so that Tate could get it back to the uHaul rental place as soon as possible. Then we would put all the equipment back into the barn that Tate kept everything in on his property, and only then were we allowed to go home. This would usually be around one thirty or two in the morning some times. So figure the day of a show you were running around for a solid fourteen or fifteen hours at least between traveling to the venue, setting up for the show, doing the show, tearing down the set up for the show, and unloading and putting away the equipment for the show. And if that isn't bad enough, some day's I wouldn't get home from the show till about two thirty in the morning and I'd have to get up for work the next day at like ten o'clock in the morning. So until I ate something, showered, and got ready for bed, It would be about three or four o'clock in the morning before I'd even get to crawl into bed after the show.

    So needless to say exhaustion after the show was

real! Also all that action in a day made a man pretty hungry and usually, sure if you were lucky you could fit a piece of pizza or a burger or two from the concession stand into the mix, but most of the time after lunch you didn't really get anything to eat. So by the time you got home you were not only tired as heck but starving as well. Most people don't realize just how much goes into being a part of the industry. There's a lot more two it then you see on television. What you see on television isn't even half of what those men and women go through on the daily and they usually aren't required to set up and tear down for the show like those of us on the indies are.

## CHAPTER VI

## REFEREEING

In June of 2019 Tate told us that we were invited to do a privet show at a family reunion for Bobby Kruger's family. None of the referee's for ACW could make the privet show so Tate told me that I was going to get my first taste of being a referee inside the ring. Sure it was just a privet show but I couldn't wait. I was thinking to myself, "I'm gonna go in there, and I'm gonna kill it. I'm gonna be awesome, It's gonna be amazing!" We only set up the ring and we used the back of the uHaul as a backstage area.

Before the show after everything was set up I went in search for Tate. When I found him I told him that I didn't want to use my real name to referee under and that I'd like to use the name Axl Fox. Tate said, "The fans are gonna call you A**hole Fox." I was thinking to myself and so badly wanted to say to him, "OK, And we use to chant Twisted Taint when you were a bad guy and were in the ring." But again I had a lot of respect for Tate so of course I didn't say that. Tate told me that it was alright for me to use Axl Fox as a ring name and told me to inform the ring announcer Carolina Jim.

I told Carolina Jim that I wanted to be announced as Axl Fox and he made a not of it in his notes for the show. When it came time for the show to begin beings I was the only referee I went out to the ring and just stayed out in the ring instead of coming backstage after every match. The show intro began and I got into position backstage to make my way to the ring. After the intro ended I walked out as Carolina Jim began to announce the first match. It felt unreal to hear Carolina Jim say, "Your referee for the evening, Aaaaaaaaxl Fooooox!" I didn't even have my referee gear yet, I was rocking an ACW shirt and track pants with a pair of cheap sneakers I got from Walmart.

I was so glad this was only a privet show and that it wasn't being recorded, at least not by the promotion itself anyway. I was absolutely terrible in the ring. My counting was way to fast and inconstant, My movement in the ring was practically a liability in itself, and my ring awareness was nonexistent as so much as a passing bird would distract me. I had so much to learn and to work on yet. I was definitely anything but ready to be in that ring let alone be the law inside that ring. I sucked so bad I wouldn't even have respected my authority in that ring if I

## REF AXL FOX

was one of the wrestlers.

About 2 months later in August of 2019, Tate would tell me that I was going to be give a match or two on the show to referee. This was my big moment to shine, I would be officially making my Atomic Championship Wrestling debut as a referee. A few days prior to the show Tate had given me a referee shirt that was about three sizes to big for me. This thing looked like a dress on me, I knew if I didn't want to look goofy that I'd better tuck my shirt into my pants. By now I was rocking the classic zebra stripes aka a black and white striped referee shirt, a black pair of dress pants, but I refused to wear the classic dress shoes so I continued to wear my cheap black and white sneakers from Walmart and I also had a pair of AMA high impact wrestling knee pads. I was pumped to go out there and be part of the show.

My first official ACW show as a referee was also a show we traveled for. The show was in Reading, Pennsylvania at the Reverb Nightclub. At the time my vehicle, a Vento Zip Li 50cc motor scooter had broken down on me so I had no way to the show so Tate told me I could ride in the uHaul with him. I was kind of glad I had to get a ride to the show as the Reverb Nightclub isn't exactly in the best part of the city of Reading. The nightclub is on $9^{th}$ street and just two blocks over on $11^{th}$ street is where the "lady's of the night" if you catch my drift, frequent the streets. I remember one ACW show I attended at the Reverb as a fan I did ride my scooter to the show and I went north on $9^{th}$ street instead of going south and I ended up in the REALLY bad part of Reading, Pennsylvania.

I know this because a block or two after my wrong turn I saw one cop car, then another cop car and I was like, "They got somebody!" I then saw a white van that had the word, "Coroner" on the side of it and a third cop car parked in front of it. I was like, "Nope, I'm turning around!" I went the other way and eventually found the Reverb. I like to joke with people now and tell them I know where to find a hooker in the city of Reading. Most people don't believe me and then when I tell them are surprised that I actually know where to find a hooker in the city of Reading.

Anyway, Back to my story of that particular show at the Reverb. After the show was over, one of the other guys on the roster needed a ride as well. Tate totally forgot he gave me a ride in the uHaul and he told this guy he could ride in the uHaul. Tate had to scramble around to try and find me a ride home and eventually he asked LuFisto if she could give me a ride home. Part of me was freaking out but another part of me was nervous as heck because one of the best female wrestlers in the world as going to give me, a noob to the industry a ride home. This would be when I learned just how big a fan of Avenged Sevenfold that LuFisto is and that she has GREAT taste in music.

The featured superstars for our show that night was none other that ECW Legend The Sandman and

## *REF AXL FOX*

WWE Legend Gillberg. I was super excited as The Sandman is one of my greatest inspirations when it comes to professional wrestling. He was one of the guys who made me want to watch ECW. Never in a million years did I ever think I'd be in the same locker room, working the same show as The Sandman of all people. I'd be lying if I didn't say part of me wanted to just go full out mark and fan boy out completely. "Mark" is professional wrestling term used to describe fan who buys way to much into the characters, story lines, and emotions of professional wrestling.

My first match that I would get to referee would be a Triple Threat Match for the ACW Tri State Championship. The Tri State Championship was one of the mid-card title of Atomic Championship Wrestling. I was absolutely shocked when I found out that not only was my very first match to referee a Triple Threat Match, but also it was a Championship Match. I totally didn't expect to be given this much responsibility right out the gate. To know that not only was I being trusted to keep more then two guys under control but to know I was trusted officiating a match that would effect the championship history of ACW was a complete honor to me. I was so ready to go out there and be the best professional wrestling referee in the history of the industry.

I had a few people within the professional wrestling industry that I looked up to for inspiration as a professional wrestling referee. I remember growing up always watching Earl Hebner in WWE and later in TNA and in my books he was and still is an absolute legend when it comes to notable referees in the industry. He almost reminded me of Ric Flair only the referee version of Ric Flair. Earl Hebner was always sliding around the ring and when it came to his authority in that ring, You respected him no questions asked. I also remember how he use to be part of story lines in wrestling as well. I remember one story line when he was in TNA where "The Beautiful People" consisting of Lacey Von Erich, Velvet Sky, and Madison Rayne would try to use their good looks and attraction to get Earl Hebner to show them favoritism in their matches. If memory serves me correctly I do believe Earl Hebner was also the referee who officiated the infamous Montreal Screw job in WWE between Bret "Hitman" Hart and Shawn Micheals.

    A more modern influence of mine when it comes to professional wrestling referees is the greatest female referees of all time, the absolute G.O.A.T of refereeing Aubrey Edwards from AEW. Aubrey is the main reason I didn't use my real name to referee under. Aubrey's real name is Brittany but she doesn't referee with that name. On an episode of *"Talk Is Jericho"* Aubrey revealed the two main reason why she doesn't use her real name to referee. She didn't want their to be confusion with professional wrestler Britt Baker who also wrestles for AEW. She also says her ring name was inspired by her late father.

    I decided not to use my real name to referee

## *REF AXL FOX*

because Jamie Senegal was also working with Atomic Championship Wrestling. It was confusing enough when in training or backstage someone would go, "Hey Jaime" or "Jamie" and both myself as well as Jamie Senegal would turn our heads of answer. Then the person would have to clarify which Jamie they were talking to. Most people assume that I chose the name Axl because I'm this huge fan of Guns N' Roses front man Axl Rose. I chose the name Axl because I've always liked that name especially when it's spelled Axl instead of Axel. The last name Fox also is because I always liked the surname Fox.

The biggest inspiration for my professional wrestling career as a referee though came from Danny Davis who refereed in the WWF in the 80's into the mid 90's. Danny was for the most part a referee but in the mid 80's be began to wrestle as well under the ring name Mr. X wearing a mask so nobody would realize his true identity. After this time Danny Davis would become known as "Dangerous" Danny Davis due to his reputation of being a biased referee, being accused of accepting bribes, as well as showing favoritism in the ring. At one point I pitched the idea to Tate for me to use my real life relation with "Coach" Dan Marks as a story line to my showing favoritism to the wrestler that Dan managed by the name of Wisly Jaccinor. My idea was that for a few shows I would show favoritism to Wesley and then it come to surface that Dan and I had an agreement since we were related. Basically my idea was shot down and rejected and the "Commissioner" of ACW Max Tempest told me that, "Referee's don't have gimmicks!"

## *JAIME MOYER*

I thought to myself, "Yes they do, Obviously you never watch Earl Hebner or "Dangerous" Danny Davis, as well as a plethora of other great referee's in professional wrestling history." I also wanted to say to Max, "You're the Commissioner, And Commissioner's don't get involved in matches yet you've been involved in quite a few matches in ACW history." Of course I didn't thought because showing disrespect like that to the Commissioner of all people would be ground for me to be pulled from the show as well as suspended at least if not worse fired from ACW. During this time before the show I'd get dressed in the bathroom instead of in the backstage area with everyone else. I never really did feel comfortable in a locker room setting, even when I was in school I absolutely HATED getting dressed for gym class. Once I was dressed I would go back to the backstage area and usually found a corner to sit in and listen to my music.

I would listen to my music as a method to keep my anxiety from getting the best of me prior to the show. During one show we had at the Stevens Fire Hall in Stevens, Pennsylvania the Senior Referee of ACW Zack Carlucci aka "Beetle Juice" has come up to me. I took out one of my headphones and he said to me, "You think you're better then me?" Confused by his accusations I replied, "No." He said, "Well then when you come into the locker room you need to introduce yourself to the people you don't know and say Hello to the people you do know." This was my first lesson in locker room etiquette.

## *REF AXL FOX*

I had a lot of respect for Zack as well as at one show he noticed I was very nervous and it showed in the ring. He told me that I have a lot of potential and gave me some tips and pointers as to how I could improve. So from that point on, Whenever I first entered the locker room I was greet everyone and introduce myself to those I didn't yet know. My rule was if you introduced yourself to me as, "Hi, My names *insert ring name*" then I would tell my name is Axl. But if you introduced yourself as, "Hi, My name is *insert not your ring name* then I would tell you my name is Jaime. I really liked the people who would introduce themselves by saying, "Hi, My names *insert ring name,* but you can call me *insert not ring name.*

Leading up to our show in February of 2019 once again at the Reverb Nightclub in Reading, Pennsylvania, I began to have pain in my shoulder as well as in my neck. The right side of my neck was so swollen it looked like Brock Lesnars neck when he was in his prime int the early 2000's. After that show I went to the doctor to get it checked out as the pain and swelling wasn't getting any better. The doctor did some tests and some imagery work and diagnosed me with rotator cuff impingement syndrome as well as muscle spasms in my neck as a result of the impingement in my rotator cuff. Just hearing the word rotator cuff I knew it was anything but good. The doctor put me in a sling for the next four weeks and told me it wouldn't be a good idea to referee for a bit as the continuous motions and movements of refereeing was a major factor in what was going on.

## *JAIME MOYER*

Rotator Cuff Impingement Syndrome is also known as Rotator Cuff Tendinitis which happens when the top outer edge of your shoulder blades pinches the rotator cuff beneath it causing the tendon to become irritated or damaged to the point the rotator cuff becomes inflamed as swells with fluid causing pain. You're lucky if treatment is only taking a break from physical activities for a while and icing it. Some people even have to do physical therapy. But the not so lucky people have to have rotator cuff surgery which is never on anyone's bingo card to say the least. So now that I was rocking a sling for a few weeks I couldn't train and even worse I had to sit out our next show. This was the first time I would be sidelined with an injury in my professional wrestling career.

It sucked, I hated it, I just wanted to rip my sling off and go out there and do what I enjoyed doing. This wasn't even an injury related to my career in professional wrestling. It was the result of that time I kicked Craig in the face when he was going to Tombstone Piledrive me in the backyard and ended up dropping me on the back of my neck breaking my collar bone and shoulder blade when I was a teenager, and then a year later breaking my humerus proximal aspect in lacrosse coming back to haunt me. But I knew that unlike when I was a teenager and didn't listen to the doctor regarding my collar bone and shoulder blade injury that it was best to listen to the doctor. Especially if I wanted to continue my career as a professional wrestling referee. So I helped the best I could with setting up for the show and then sat backstage during the show watching from the back.

    This diagnosis would haunt me over and over again throughout my career. I became so familiar with the people at the physical therapy place I went to that I know probably 99% of them on a first name basis. At one point my doctor had told me that if I continued having issues with my rotator cuff being impinged that he might recommend we look into getting rotator cuff surgery. This was NOT what I wanted to hear, In fact it was the LAST thing I wanted to hear. Rotator Cuff surgery is usually the end of the road when it comes to any athletes career, not just in professional wrestling. The only thing worse then a rotator cuff injury I can think of would probably be an ACL and/or MCL injury.

    One more thing I had on my bucket list for my career was to work in another promotion besides ACW. Don't get me wrong ACW was great but limiting my career to only working in ACW would limit my legacy to only ACW. I had got in touch with Ray Torres from Regional Championship Wrestling and offered to work for him at RCW. Ray would eventually message me back and offer me not one but two dates that RCW had shows that he wanted me to work. Prior to this I had attended a couple RCW shows and at the show I attended prior to being offered work by RCW I had helped set up and tear down for the show.

    If memory serves me correctly Ray even told me to bring my referee gear to the show and he'd see about giving me a spot on the card. Due to the Corona Virus shutting everything down, the two dates I was booked to work for RCW ultimately got canceled along with my chance to cross yet another thing off my professional wrestling referee bucket list. I guess one could argue though that since I did set up and tear down for an RCW show that technically I did work for another promotion just not as a referee. I was so pumped to work those two dates for RCW, I felt so great when Ray contacted me to book me for those two shows. To have it all ripped away though was frustrating and depressing to say the least. So to say my career as a professional wrestling referee was smooth sailing is anything but true.

## CHAPTER VII

## TNA

While I was refereeing on the indies, I still watched professional wrestling on television religiously. I watched WWE Raw on Mondays, WWE NXT on Tuesdays, AEW Dynamite on Wednesdays, TNA Impact on Thursdays, WWE SmackDown on Fridays, AEW Collision on Saturdays and your occasionally WWE pay-per-view, and your occasion WWE NXT pay-per-view on Sundays. TNA has always been one of my favorite promotions and in my honestly opinion I feel they have been on top of the wrestling food chain for a while now. I've been subscribed to their YouTube channel for over 2 years now. I tend to be very vocal on their live stream of their shows. In January of 2022 a faction known as Honor No More ran rapid through TNA.

Everyone in the live stream chat as well as in the crowd in attendance would boo them heavily. I however happened to be a big fan of them as the faction contained one of my all time favorite teams in professional wrestling under the Ring Of Honor brand known as The Kingdom. The Kingdom was made up of Matt Taven, Mike Bennett, and Maria Kanellis formally Maria from WWE. So I would always type things into the chat in support of Honor No More and whoever monitored the chat for TNA would occasionally say things along the lines of how disappointing it is that such a longtime fan like myself would turn out to be a fan of Honor No More. At one point they even silenced me from chatting in the live stream for like a week or two so that I could show my support for Honor No More. They even made it a point to announce in the chat that I had been silenced from chatting.

Before I get to that though, I remember Vita VonStarr would always give me a hard time about being a fan of The Kingdom in Ring Of Honor. She worked for Ring Of Honor but she was part of a faction known as The Righteous which was lead by Vinny Marseglia along side Tyler Bateman and Vita VonStarr. Vita would tell me that I should be a fan of The Righteous instead of "Following The Trend" and being a fan of The Kingdom. Especially during the feud between The Righteous and The Kingdom in Ring Of Honor. Honestly unarguably one of the greatest rivalries in ROH History if you want my true opinion on it. But like I said, The Kingdom was my favorite faction of all time in Ring Of Honor.
Now, Honor No More besides being comprised of Matt Taven, Mike Kanellis and Maria Kanellis aka The Kingdom, and was also comprised of Vinny Marseglia, Kenny King, Eddie Edwards, and PCO. I then began

joking with Vita that I was finally a fan of Vinny like she always wanted. Not going to lie, I always saw Vinny joining Impact Wrestling as the perfect opportunity for Vita VonStarr to get her foot in the door with Impact but that never happened. I guess Impact Wrestling had other ideas other then bringing The Righteous to Impact Wrestling. Now lets get to the good stuff, Where I become known as a "Heel Fan" and an "Insider Traitor" to Impact Wrestling. Also can't forget the opportunity of a lifetime I was given either by Impact Wrestling.

The first time Impact Wrestling silenced me in the chat was January 27th, 2022 when they posted "@Axl Fox bro" as well as "Should I put Impact Insider Traitor @Axl Fox in "Time Out!"" Then posting, "Axl Fox is in TIME OUT" after finding out I supported Honor No More. Then a month later on February 24th, 2022 I was silenced a second time and they posted, "@Axl Fox is the biggest heel fan INSIDER" and then said, "@AxlFox it was for your own good, Daddio." Ultimate Insiders where what they called their top tier supporters on YouTube which like I said I have been subscribed to for over two years now. The third time Impact Wrestling silenced me in the chat was on June 2nd, 2022 and they posted in the chat, "Okay, Axl is gone for a few minutes – everyone talk crap about Honor No More." I took a screenshot of both announcements in the chat and posted it on my Instagram and even tagged all the members of Honor No More.

The first and third posts I made about being silenced in the chat by Impact Wrestling, Matt Taven himself liked them on Instagram. I was really making a name for myself among the Impact Wrestling community as a true heel fan, a traitor to the TNA Impact Wrestling community. For at least five months Impact Wrestling and myself kept this going without ever planning it. Not once did I reach out to them or they reach out to me and ask to have a set something up within their live stream. I was was a lot of fun though. And having Matt Taven himself interact with my posts about it all was even sweeter.

    I did mention a few times in the live stream chats of Impact Wrestling that I was a referee on the independent circuit and quite a few times the moderator of the Impact Wrestling YouTube channel had invited me to come out to Nashville, Tennessee for a tryout with Impact Wrestling. Now don't get me wrong I would have loved to work for TNA as a referee, but I knew I shouldn't even be working the indies as a referee with my seizure disorder. I had been involved in the industry since November 2018 without my neurologist knowing anything about it. If he did find out about it, I'm sure he would have shut it down real quick as he shot the idea of it originally down faster then ever. Also beings I live in Denver, Pennsylvania and Nashville, Tennessee is over 750 miles away I knew that it would be a lot to commit to just to go to the tryout. And what if I did end up getting signed?

    I don't drive because of extreme anxiety stemming from my near fatal car crash in 2016, so how exactly was I going to get their let alone travel from show to show if I do get signed? Then there's the fact I have a solid  job here in Pennsylvania that I love working in a nursing and rehabilitation facility. Did I really want to leave that and start a new life in Nashville? Also there's the fact I have a nice apartment here in Pennsylvania here the rent is insanely cheap, If I were to pack up and move to Nashville I guarantee my rent wouldn't be as low as it is now. And of course you can't forget the factor of my family and friends here in Pennsylvania, I don't know anybody in Nashville, I have no family in Nashville. So I'd be moving miles away from everyone I know and love just work a job where I don't know when the next time I'd see my family and friends again would be.

 Sure you're probably sitting there saying to yourself, "Bro, Are you stupid, Lots of people in the professional wrestling industry dream of this moment!" And you're one hundred percent right to put that on the table. But I've never really been good when it comes to the What If's in life. Worry is a key factor when it comes to my anxiety disorder and my mental health. It always seems to get the best of me, every time. I just couldn't see leaving everything I know and love here in Pennsylvania to pursue a life that seems so glamorous but is full of the unknown.

 I am absolutely grateful for the opportunity that Impact Wrestling offered me to come out to Nashville for a tryout. But looking at how my anxiety effected me on the indies, I just don't feel like it would be worth it. I mean I got super nervous to the point I was shaking during the Texas Bullrope Match in front of maybe a hundred to one hundred and fifty people. How in the heck was I going to compose myself in front of a crown of tens of thousands of people? Sometimes in life it's just best to go with your gut and ignore what your heart and your head is telling you. It takes a bigger person to admit when the water is a bit to deep and turn back, then it does to swim out even further only to be swept under and dragged out to sea by the current.

## Chapter VIII

## The Highlight Reel

Personally I feel like when it comes to the highlights of my career, I don't have to think very hard to come up with at least a few. Of course there's my very first match in August of 2019 at the Reverb. A Triple Threat Match for the ACW Tri State Championship. The nerves and anxiety of it all absolutely ate me alive that night. I walked through the curtain confident as can be but once the bell rang to start the match, That confidence went right out the window. Everything I learned up to that point and everything I knew left, I looked absolutely ridiculous in that ring.

It might have even been a Fatal 4 Way Match. All I remember is at one point all the wrestlers left the ring and I was the only one in the ring. The wrestlers began running around the ring like it was a race or something. I was so confused as to what was going on, I almost forgot to start counting them out. When I did start the count, I counted way to fast. I think I even had to stop counting because I got to nine and they weren't yet in the ring but the match wasn't scheduled to end via count out of any kind.

Another notable match in my career happened at a show at the Stevens Fire Hall in Stevens, Pennsylvania. It was the very first match under the Rouge Women Warriors banner of Atomic Championship Wrestling that I refereed. Rouge Women Warriors was what ACW called their Women's division. I was assigned the match between Queen Aminata taking on Vita Von Star. Before the match I checked the women to make sure they didn't have any illegal objects hidden in their gear. I went to check Queen Aminata and after I checked her elbow pads and went to check her knee pads she turned around a stuck her butt out at me. I'd be lying if I said this didn't catch me off guard a little bit as she didn't tell me prior to the match she was going to do this.

I stepped back and told her, "Hey, I'm the referee, I'm just trying to do my job." Then I heard someone from the crowd yell, "That's the most action he's probably gotten in his lifetime!" At this point I was completely embarrassed as my mom was sitting right there in the front row as well. Queen Aminata finally let me check her knee pads and I called for the bell to be rung starting the match. This would also be the first time I refereed a match for a wrestler in the big leagues as Vita VonStarr was a female superstar for Ring Of Honor in Philadelphia,

## *REF AXL FOX*

Pennsylvania. Queen Aminata would eventually after this go onto the big leagues herself and currently works for All Elite Wrestling as part of their women's division.

One show we had at the Stevens Fire Hall I remember I was refereeing a match with in my opinion a pure legend in the indie wrestling scene "The Deathmatch Guardian" Stockade. I forget who exactly he was facing but I do remember after the match I held up his hand in victory and then I heard the music of Jay Savage hit and out came Jay Savage. Now Stockade is a big solid boy, and Jay Savage well lets just say he works shows with a promotion called Midgets With Attitude but is pretty built himself. I was so confused as to what was going on as I had no prior knowledge of any post match interference scheduled to take place. Jay got in the ring and stood toe to toe with Stockade for a moment and then split the uprights, If your confused, He kicked Stockade in the nuts and then left the ring. Now as a referee I'm expected to be impartial but in a moment like this, How do you be impartial and not bust out in laughter?

I mean a literal midget just kicked a man easily five times his size in the nuts, and I'm supposed to be professional and not laugh. I held my composure the best I could but little did I know this would lead up to the next month a match between Jay Savage and Stockade and guess who was assigned that match as the referee? That's right, I would be assigned that match. It was a pretty easy match to referee as it was basically just Stockade tossing Jay around like a rag doll for most the match and Jay getting a few shots in where he could, but if memory serves me correctly Stockade won that match. I just can't forget how in the moment when Jay first came out and kicked Stockade in the nuts I thought to myself, "What the heck is this!"

A match that I also really enjoyed because it gave me the opportunity to cross something off my professional wrestling bucket list as a referee. This show happened in July of 2020 at a show we ran outdoors due to the Corona Virus pandemic, at the Orioles Home Association, Nest 147 in Newmanstown, Pennsylvania. This was another match between Bones and Scotty Jeffferies for the ACW Tri State Championship. I wanted to take a ref bump so badly. So I pitched the idea to Bones and Scotty and Scotty told me to talk to Tate knowing I have a seizure disorder. So I went and found Tate and asked him if I could take a ref bump, and Tate said, "Absolutely not!"

I begged him and pleaded with him to let me do it and eventually he agreed with the understanding that if anything happened he as well as Scotty and Bones wouldn't be able to be held liable. Tate and I went back to Scotty and Bones and Tate told them he ok'ed the spot and that he wants to know EXACTLY what was going to take place and that absolutely no head shots would be allowed. Scotty had come up with the idea that he have Bones in the corner and I start my count to five but at four I shoves Scotty back off Bones. With Bones still in the corner Scotty would go to the opposite ring corner and run at Bones after I checked on Bones. Bones would pull me

## REF AXL FOX

into the corner as he moved out of the corner so that I would take a splash from Scotty instead of him. Scotty would hit me with a splash in the corner and I would fall to the mat looking like I was knocked out giving Bones enough time to hit Scotty with brass knuckles.

Tate approved of the spot and confirmed with me that this was indeed what I wanted to do. I told him I did want to do it, After all Scotty was someone I respected and trusted more then anybody in ACW and by this point I had spent most of my career up to this point officiating his matches. We went out there and when it came time to do the spot we planned it went off perfectly. After Bones hit Scotty with the brass knuckles he checked them out of the ring and shock me as e covered Scotty yelling, "Do your job ref!" I acted like I came to groggy as ever and began to count 1...2...3, I got up still selling that I was sore from the splash in the corner and called for the bell to be rung ending the match. I raised Bones hand in victory and handed him his ACW Tri State Championship and still selling the splash in the corner I fumbled back to the backstage area where Tate even complimented me on how good I sold the splash in the corner to make it look believable that I had been knocked out.

At one point Tate was part of a story line where he was suspended from ACW and wasn't to be at the show. We were told Tate was going to show up and get in the ring and all us referee's were to go out to the ring and tell Tate he had to leave. Tate would refuse so we would detain him and escort him out of the building. When it came time for that portion of the show, Tate went out to the ring and began to cut a promo. Commissioner Max Tempest came out and asked Tate what in the heck he was doing at the show. Max would then call for security and that was our que to come out and remove Tate from the building.

    I told Tate, "Turn around and put your hands behind your back!" Of course being the heel he was at the time he laughed at me an resisted a bit before following our instructions. We cuffed Tate up and helped him out of the ring and out of the building as everyone cheered. Little did they know we simply escorted Tate outside and then uncuffed him but that's besides the point. But the moral of the story here is I got to "arrest" my wrestling trainer, the promoter of ACW, and the owner of ACW and kick him out of his own show essentially. Not many people get that kind of luxury!

    My absolute favorite match that I got to referee was again at a show at the Reverb in Reading, Pennsylvania in February of 2020. It was a Texas Bullrope Match between Bones and Scotty Jefferies again for the ACW Tri State Championship. This would be only the second Texas Bullrope Match in the history of Atomic Championship Wrestling so it was an incredible honor for me to be assigned this match to referee. Not going to lie though, It was a lot to handle. I had to go out with the Bullrope and when Bones and Scotty entered the ring I have to fasten the rope to their wrists. I was so nervous and anxious that as I was trying to snap the strap at the one end of the rope around Scottys wrist, I was shaking so badly the rope kept slipping out of my hand.

Scotty said, "Dude, Why you so shaky?" I said, "I'm nervous a hell, man!" He said, "Well just calm down, You'll be fine." After securing the bullrope to the wrists of Scotty and Bones I called for the bell to be rung starting the match. I was so focused on not looking stupid in the ring and doing a good job that I almost forgot to be aware of where the rope was and not tripping over the rope myself. At one point Bones and Scotty went outside the ring and I started to count and someone in the crowed yelled, "It's No DQ, There are not count outs, stupid!" I was like, "Oh yeah, I forgot" and I stopped counting.

Now a Texas Bullrope Match can only be won when a wrestler touches all four corners of the ring without interruption. At one point one of the guys had touches one ring post more then I had counted and had to correct me on how many ring posts the touched. During the match the rope ended up breaking at one point and I believe it was Scottys end, so he had to hold the rope which I tried to duck tape it to his wrist. I got in a lot of trouble from Tate after the show because I had posted about the match on Instagram and put how the rope broke and Tate told me that was "disrespectful" and that I "shouldn't be bashing the promotion online." It wasn't my intention to bash ACW, I was just frustrated that the rope broke. But I saw Tates point so I went onto the post and I re-captioned it with a more respectful caption.

*JAIME MOYER*

## CHAPTER IX

## THE REFOLUTION

In addition to not using my birth given name to referee under, I had the idea to bring back the infamous referee stunner. If you've ever played any of the old school wrestling games, you know exactly what I'm talking about. You'd hit the referee a few times and then after a while he would hit you with a stunner of all stunners. The closest thing to this that I saw in ACW was a female referee by the name of Tanya had come to one of the ACW shows after her time with the company and Tate offered her a spot on the card. The one wrestler in the match just refused to listen to anything she said and kept testing her patients and she slapped him clear across the face and I swear you could see the taste fly out of his mouth. I never did find the right opportunity to do a referee stunner during my time with ACW though.

Also I knew that professional wrestling referees typically don't have long hair or fancy haircuts and they generally are clean shaven. I most definitely wasn't going to shave my facial hair and look like a twelve year old, but also I at the time was rocking a small mohawk that I thought was pretty cool. Eventually I did give in and end up shaving my head though no one had ever said anything to me about my appearance. I was also about 6ft 3in tall which was monstrous for a professional wrestling referee. I even found out later on down the road that WWE actually has a rule that you can be a referee if your over 6ft tall because they don't want the referees overshadowing the talent in the ring. So there went any hopes I did have of being a referee in the WWE even though I always said I'd never be a referee in WWE and that I'd rather be a referee in TNA instead.

Another thing that was on my professional wrestling bucket list of things to do to change the game when it came to refereeing was that I wanted to make merchandise. I began looking into places online, I wasn't able to make a shop on places like Pro Wrestling Tee's because I didn't have a big enough fan base. Eventually I would come across a site called Bonfire where I could not only sell my merchandise but I could also create it myself. I had the BEST idea for my first shirt, The fans like to chant at you as a referee things along the lines of, "You can't count" or "Do you even know what comes after two?" So, Why not play off that? So I made a shirt that says, *"1...2...? What Comes After 2?"*

## *REF AXL FOX*

    I of course ordered one for myself and I began to wear it to every show so that the fans could see and hopefully ask me how they to can have one. Little did I know that not everyone would find my idea to make merchandise as cool and game changing as I did. I asked Tate if I could set up a merchandise table at the shows and he told me, "Referees don't sell merch!" Larry, I believe it was, a fellow referee told me, "I wouldn't want to wear a shirt with all that text on it and no graphic." I didn't let that stop me from making more merchandise though, My next shirt would say, *"No Fox Given"*, See what I did there in place of the F word I put Fox cause they sound similar. Referees are to be the authority in the ring so I figured it also played into that I won't take no crap from anybody attitude of a true professional wrestling referee.

    After that I saw Bonfire had "jersey style" shirts and I thought the looked pretty cool. I put the word REFEREE on the front with a clip art picture of a referee on it and then on the back it has "*Axl Fox*", and where the name goes and the number is none other then *123*. The next shirt I would make would feature a clip art picture of a championship title belt and another clip art picture of a zebra's head over top of it. Then the words, "Zebra Gang" in reference to referee's being called zebra's or the stripes on their shirts being refereed to as zebra stripes. It's kind of a referee thing, You either get or you don't. That was the most recent shirt that I made. I also applied some of these designs to things like coffee mugs because, when have you ever seen a professional wrestler selling coffee mugs as part of their merchandise?

## *JAIME MOYER*

     In the off chance that you're sitting there and wondering, "Well where can I get these shirts you speak of?" The answer is quite simple, go to bonfire.com/store/refaxlfox to get your Ref Axl Fox merchandise today! It's still my goal to change the game forever when it comes to refereeing and that still involves making referee merchandise a thing. Why should the wrestlers get all the fun promoting themselves outside the ring? In my opinion, Referee's are one of the most underrated and under-recognized people in the professional wrestling industry. Early in this chapter I told you about some of the best professional wrestling referee's that influence me, which proves that referee's do make an impact in this industry as well.

## CHAPTER X

## RETIREMENT

While I was on the shelf recovering and rehabbing the muscle spasms in my trap muscle as well as the impingement in my rotator cuff the world would be shut down due to growing concern over the Corona Virus. This would mean that the sports entertainment world as a whole, not just pro wrestling, wouldn't be allowed to performed in front of a live audience. Promotions such as TNA and AEW would perform in empty arenas, while WWE put together a way the fans could still be a part of the show without being physically in attendance. They would call this idea, "The Tunderdome" and essentially it was a bunch of monitors that would live stream the fans from their homes via webcam all around the arena. For smaller promotions such as Atomic Championship Wrestling it was just to hard to make shows work under the strict conditions of the Center for Disease Control also known as the CDC. Most of the indie promotions where forced to shut their doors during this time which meant a loss of profit for many.

Tate stayed on top of things when it came to what the CDC was saying regarding the Corona Virus pandemic and the rules and regulations the CDC had in place in regards to running live shows again. In July of 2020, Five months after I began having issues with my neck and shoulder, Tate would be told that we could run a live show but it had to be outdoors, only so many people could be there which included fans, talent, staff, etc The ring had to be wiped down and sanitized after every match, everyone had to wear masks but wrestlers could remove their mask once they were in the ring. And a representative from the state health organization had to be in attendance, as well as a slue of other quite frankly frustrating and obnoxious rules and regulations. Referee's had to keep their masks on which was an absolute nightmare for me considering with all the running around I had to do in the ring, It was hard enough to breath thanks to my bad heart valve. I was still excited to make my return from my injury though as the past five months had felt like five years since I last refereed a match.

Ultimately after that show, Tate decided it was just to much of a hassle to start running shows again if we had to do all that just to have a show. Tate would go back to checking in with the CDC to see weather or not it was safe to run shows again or not, regardless of the fact that at this point every other promotion was running shows.

## *REF AXL FOX*

Once other promotions began opening their doors and running shows again a good portion of the ACW roster decided to go elsewhere to continue their careers. I however decided to stay loyal to ACW and stay hopeful that we to would be able to do shows again as well. I waited and waited and every so often would even reach out to Tate to see if he had any word on when we could expect to run shows again. Over two years later we still weren't running shows because Tate said everyone had jumped ship to other promotions.

    The Corona Virus pandemic wouldn't be the thing that ultimately led to my decision to hang it up when it came to being a professional wrestling referee though. In the end of April 2023 I was skateboarding with a friend of mine at a local skate park. I decided to do a front side board slide down the railing of the staircase that was in the park. It was only about three stairs high but they were very long and wide steps. About halfway down the railing my right foot came off my board and to keep myself from falling I put my foot on the ground and it rolled inward. I limped over to a ledge of the skate park and sat down taking my shoe off to let my foot breath a bit.

    My friend asked if I was alright and I told him, "I think I broke my foot." He said, "You mean like give it three days and you'll be fine, broke your foot, or You need to go to the hospital, broke your foot?" I said, "I need to go to the hospital, broke my foot!" My friend not thinking I was being serious said, "You'll be fine, just walk it off." Thinking to myself, "Maybe I am being over dramatic" I got up and tried to walk and all I could feel was excruciating pain in my foot. I sat back down and said to my friend, "Yeah, It's definitely broke!"

My friend said, "Alright, Do you want to go to the hospital or to urgent care. I told him I'd prefer to go to urgent care cause I didn't feel like spending the rest of the day waiting in the emergency room to be told what I already know. After all I couldn't even walk to the car so I had to literally sit on my skateboard and push with my hands and my one good foot through the grass to the parking lot where the car was parked. My friend dropped me off at urgent care and helped me inside. Once I got called back from the waiting room the doctor just looking at my foot confirmed that I indeed broke my foot but x-rays where required in order to tell exactly how I broke my foot. Even the x-rays didn't take a rocket scientist to see that my foot was indeed broken.

The diagnosis was a two millimeter break in the base of the fifth metatarsal in my right foot. In simpler terms I broke the very back of my little toe where your toe connects to your foot. The doctor fitted met with a soft cast and a set of crutches and sent me on my way with orders to follow up with an Orthopedic doctor to be fitted for an air cast. Thankfully wrestling still wasn't happening so I didn't have to worry about being on the shelf again and missing any shows. Two months later I would be free from the air cast but the doctor had told me that the break in my foot hadn't properly healed. He told me basically that where the break was instead of new bone forming like he thought was happening, scare tissue had filled the break meaning my foot most likely will never heal fully.

      I knew this was bad news as not only did I rely on my feet to perform the sickest referee slide I could in the ring, I also needed my feet to play softball. To be honest I was a lot better at softball then I was a refereeing so I made the decision to hang up the zebra stripes so I could continue playing softball. I officially announced my retirement from professional wrestling as a referee via a post on Instagram featuring a photo of all my referee gear neatly folded and stacked on top of each other and a caption explaining that I was calling it quits from refereeing in professional wrestling. This was honestly the hardest decision I ever had to make regarding my career as a referee, In fact it took me days just to mustard up the strength and courage to post the announcement on social media. But I knew it was not only what was best for me personally but that it was what was best for my career as well.

      After I posted the picture of my referee gear neatly folded I accompanied it with the following caption.

"I've thought long and hard about this #decision and I feel like #God has #answered my #prayers regarding this and has given me a clear #answer. So as of this day November 4th, 2023 I'm #officially hanging it up on my #career as a #ProWrestlingReferee. I'm #thankful and #grateful to @realtwistedtate for taking on the task of #training me despite my #seizuredisorder when no one else wanted to. I

## JAIME MOYER

also want to thank @ref_larryswc_ and @zackcarlucci717 for #mentoring me and taking me under their wing in #AtomicChampionshipWrestling and #RougeWomenWarriors. Thank you for allowing me to #experience what it's like to be in #ring.
Also thanks to people like @woundedowllufisto, Scotty Jefferies, @damexoxo, and so many others for giving me #advice and #tips. Thank you to the #fans who #believed in me and #supported me. I just entered this #industry at a bad time, right before the #pandemic, and because of that I never was really able to get my feet off the ground. I never intended to go far in this industry as #doctors didn't want me in it at all due to my #seizures, but just to have the experience to see what life is like on the other side of the barricade was my goal. It's crazy to think I did get offered a try out with Impact Wrestling but again I wasn't in this to go far. I leave with so many memories and friendships I'll value forever.
Before this Axl Fox was just a silly #AlterEgo I created for #socialmedia but now I can say he is a part of my life that gave me some of the best #memories of my life. I truly hope the name Axl Fox is indeed legendary among the fans of ACW and I will now return to something I love even more then my time as a #referee and that's being a fan and not just any fan, being that die hard fan sitting front row hooting and hollering!
THANK YOU TO ALL ONCE AGAIN FOR GIVING AXL FOX A TRUE PURPOSE!!!"

Fellow Referee at ACW and RWW Larry Peace, Stackade now known by the name Kaide Lothbrok, ROH's Vita VonStarr, My

## REF AXL FOX

number one fan my Mother, and another one of my biggest fans who followed me on Instagram had all liked the post, respectfully I assume. Vita VonStarr, and Hayne, who also worked for ACW as a wrestler had commented on the post. The other one of my biggest fans aside from my mom who followed me on Instagram also commented on the post, beings this fan at the time and still at this time is still a minor for protection of identity purposes I will refer to them as, "Biggest Fan #2."

VitaVonStarr: Best of luck in your future man.

Biggest Fan #2: Good luck to your future endevours.

Biggest Fan #2: Wow, thank you for what you did in the wrestling business as a ref!! You're awesome Axl & most definitely good.

Hayne: But why?

Now I know Hayne posted what he said in classic Hayne humor but I decided to take the professional route and answer the question of why in a shorter version of what I posted in the caption of the entire post.

I've been doing this since 2018 without my neurologist knowing, also I've haven't worked a show since 2020, I have rotator cuff impingement syndrome as well as recently broke my foot and it hasn't fully healed I'm not sure I'll even be able to continue playing Softball with it. Also every show my anxiety was through the roof. I respect what yall do in the ring, I enjoyed the taste of being on the other side of the barricade I did get I just came in the industry at a bad time. I worked 5 months then COVID shut everything down and my career doesn't seem to be removing from it. I have no desire to make it to the big leagues and it's difficult for me to turn off being a fan during shows. I'd be lying though if I didn't say that being a referee has given me a new respect for those who step between those ropes.

As far as what Vita VonStarr had commented I decided to stick to the professional route, and simply replied with the following.

RefAxlFox: @vitavonstarr Thanks, Loved refereeing your matches and working with you!

VitaVonStarr: @refaxlfox I appreciate that, same.

As far as responding to Biggest Fan #2, I decided to take the more open and honest route without going to far into detail on some of the things.

Thanks, I definitely have great memories and stories from my time as a referee and it's not with a heavy heart or anything that I chose to hang it up. There's a lot of politics and things that go on behind the scenes that I don't agree but have had to bite my tongue on. I got to referee some great matches with great talented men and women like @vitavonstarr, @amisylle, @jackhershey717, @damexoxo, @kaidelothbrok, and so many others. I got to meet some of my heroes like @ecwsandman and

## *REF AXL FOX*

> @screamqueendaff. I got to referee the 2nd ever Texas Bullrope Match in ACW history. My first match was a championship match. I really couldn't have asked for a better career aside from the pandemic effecting it.

To say I am content with how I retired from professional wrestling is a very large understatement. If ACW would ever start running shows again, I would most definitely like to ask Tate for some time to retire the right way. In the ring, with a hot microphone, in front of all the people who ever booed me or cheered for me, with the entire locker room surrounding the ring. I mean after all, I was never supposed to be a part of the industry in the first place. One right hit to the head and I very well could have gone into an all out seizure in the middle of the ring. And the fact that Tate knew that and still accepted the challenge of training me and eventually gave me a contract to be an official part of Atomic Championship Wrestling is something I will forever be grateful for.

I don't regret a single moment of my career as a referee. I entered the industry at a bad time, because of the pandemic I never really got the chance to get my career off the ground. I never expected to go far with my career in professional wrestling. I never desired to move on to the bigger promotions such a TNA, WWE, ROH, NJPW, AEW, etc. But I do hope and pray everyday that the fans of ACW as well as the talent of ACW remember the name Axl Fox and that I did create a least a small legacy within the promotion. I mean after all, I did referee one of only two Texas Bullrope Matches in ACW history.

## *JAIME MOYER*

Before I worked that privet show in July of 2019 where I asked Tate if I could use the name Axl Fox to referee under instead of my birth given name, Axl Fox was nothing more then an alter ego I created for myself to use online to keep from having to use my birth given name. I also created the alter ego of Axl Fox as a way to escape my personal demons that I talk about in my book, "*Fearless Over Failure*." My demons couldn't touch Axl Fox, in fact the full persona of Axl Fox is Axl "Fearless" Fox known also as "Fearless Fox." The only time my personal demons with mental illness could touch Axl "Fearless" Fox was when I was in the ring and would be anxious and worry about messing up to the point my heart felt like it was going to fall out my butt. Professional Wrestling game Axl Fox a new persona, the persona of Referee Axl Fox also known as Ref Axl Fox. Professional Wrestling gave Axl Fox live outside of my delusions from my mental health.

My career as a professional wrestling referee also gave me a new found respect not only for the industry of professional wrestling itself but for the men and women who step foot in that ring and put their bodies on the line all for the sole purpose of entertaining the fans. Dolph Ziggler once said during a promo he had on an episode of SmackDown, "Sometimes things you love, Don't love you back …!" That is most definitely the case when it comes to my career in professional wrestling. I love the absolute crap out of professional wrestling, I have since I was about ten years old, but it seems like professional wrestling just doesn't love me the same. To this day, at least twenty four years later since I began loving professional wrestling I still love it as much, if not more then I did when I was that ten year old boy. And to say I was a part of the industry I've loved since I was ten years old is absolutely mind blowing and amazing.

*JAIME MOYER*

## CHAPTER XI

## MEMORIES TO LAST A LIFETIME

My time as a professional wrestling referee may not have been as long as I imaged it to be, nor did it go the way I had originally planned for it to go. However, I'd be lying if I said it didn't give me memories that will last a lifetime, both positive and negative memories. I will cherish these memories forever. The gratitude I have for my time as a referee in the professional wrestling industry is definitely not able to be measured. Something I was never supposed to be a part of gave me some of the best memories of my life. And now I'm going to share those memories with you.

Before my first show we were out hanging fliers for the show in grocery store community boards, laundry mat community boards, restaurant windows that allowed advertising events, etc. This was one of the major was we promoted the shows to draw in a good crowd. I always found this to be fun as it somewhat had the rush of adrenaline to it that comes with doing something you shouldn't be doing. What I mean by that is people would see you taping a flier to a restaurant window or something and they'd look at you with a look like, "What is the guy doing?" Also it was a great time to bond with the others in the promotion outside of the ring. You'd say, "I'm going to put one over there" and someone else would be like, "Not if I put one there first" and it turned into a race to see who could get there first.

The night of the first show I refereed on the featured superstars to appear where Sandman from ECW and Gillberg from WWE. Gillberg was a comedy version of Goldberg from his days in WCW. Goldberg would come out with smoke and pyro so at one point Gillberg would come out with smoke and sparklers. We didn't have a smoke machine so Tate had pitched the idea of getting a fire extinguisher and having someone unload it as Gillberg came out to the ring. I told Tate, "I have an old fire extinguisher I'd like to get rid of that we can use." Tate told me to bring it to the show and I did. Unfortunately, Gillberg had informed us that he was told he could no longer do that due to the chemicals within a fire extinguisher posing a risk for chemical burns to a persons skin.

So we had to scrap that idea and I think we just ended up going with sparklers only but even forgot to do that when it came time for Gillberg to make his entrance. Gillberg ended up being a pretty cool guy and honestly funny as heck. He talked to a ton of us backstage and was just one of the most genuine people I've ever met. ACW even had it's own comedy version of WCW's Goldberg. Our version of WCW's Goldberg was ACW wrestler Mr.Chow coming out in these ridiculous black wrestling trunks and no shirt, we called him Chowberg. We even got the crowd to chant, "Chooooooowberg, Chooooooowberg!" It was honestly one of the most hilarious things I've ever seen in my time with Atomic Championship Wrestling.

    The same show I met Gillberg, I also had the honor and opportunity to meet and have my picture taken with one of my biggest influences in professional wrestling history, The Sandman! Sandman ended up being good friends with Tate and was always one call away whenever Tate needed a big name to pop up at a show. I asked Sandman if I could get a picture with him and he told me, twenty bucks!" I gave him twenty dollars and stood next to him with the biggest smile on my face. I couldn't believe I was actually standing next to Extreme Championship Wrestling Legend, The Sandman! The only way this night would get any better is if I got to referee his match, which I did not.

    Another genuine and funny person I met during my time referee for ACW was none other then former WWE superstar James Ellsworth. If that name doesn't ring a bell he was the guy with "no chin" who worked with Carmella when she won Mrs. Money In The Bank, in fact he was the one who actually unhooked the brief case for

## JAIME MOYER

her in the one Women's Money In The Bank Match that she won. Funny thing about James Ellsworth is I HATED James Ellsworth when he was in WWE. I thought he was the most untalented person on the entire roster at the time and was just a big old doofus! It was this night that my perception of James Ellsworth changed and it wasn't because I got to share a locker room with him. No, It was actually something he did that proved to me he was not a doofus but in fact a really nice guy.

I asked James if I could get a picture with him and he happily agreed. I asked him, how much is it for a picture" expecting him to say ten bucks or twenty bucks or whatever. Instead he looked at me in my referee uniform and said, "You work here right?" I said, "Yeah, I'm a referee." He said, "Well, Then for you a picture with me is FREE!" I couldn't believe my ears, This "no chin doofus" was really not going to charge me for a picture with him because I worked for the promotion he was appearing for.

After this encounter with James Ellsworth I gained a whole new respect for him. I followed him on Instagram and came to find out, DUDES A RAVENS FAN, Just like me! Now my respect for him increased even more as he is a fellow member of the Ravens Nation, Baby! I remember before the show when James was backstage talking to some of us, someone had asked him if he still talks to Carmella. He told us that he and Carmella still stay in contact and even told us she was thinking about retiring soon to focus on starting a family. So yeah, James

## *REF AXL FOX*

Ellsworth is definitely a great guy in my books.

Around the time I had gotten into the professional wrestling industry Tate was pretty close with Teddy Hart of the infamous "Hart Family" in professional wrestling. Teddy Hart is the nephew of Bret "The Hitman" Hart, He quite frequently came over to Tate's house and if we were training he would offer some of his knowledge upon us trainees. It was always funny to see Teddy roll up because he never went anywhere without his army of Persian cats. When I say army, I mean a legit army, Dude would roll up in a black Mercedes Benz with about eight to ten cats in his car, hand to God! At the time Teddy Hart seemed like a great guy. But later on, It would come out that Teddy Hart is anything but a great guy, more like a monster!

LuFisto was a regular when it came to wrestlers at Atomic Championship Wrestling. In fact later down the road when Tate would introduce a proper Women's Division known as Rouge Women Warriors, he would make LuFisto in charge of that portion of the promotion. Tate and LuFisto would for a short time be married and live together, so seeing LuFisto became a daily thing. LuFisto is a true icon when it comes to professional wrestling. One of her most famous matches is a match where she defeated Kevin Steen now known in WWE as Kevin Owens for a championship. LuFisto is known all over the world for her wrestling skills.

One moment during my career that impacted me personally didn't even happen at a show or during training or whatever. It was the tragic passing of a woman who heavily influenced my interest in professional wrestling. A woman who during her time in WCW paved the way for female wrestlers by doing things that female wrestlers during her time in WCW weren't doing. I'm talking about the late great "Scream Queen" Daffney. Daffney and her tag team partner at the time MsChief aka "The Scream Queens" where one of my favorite female tag teams in professional wrestling, of all time. Also her work managing Crowbar in World Championship Wrestling was a true game changer for female wrestlers from that point on. I got the opportunity in 2017 at an Atomic Championship Wrestling show to meet Daffney and get my picture taken with her.

    In 2021, Shannon Spurill aka Daffney would take to social media and on a live stream read what ultimately was a suicide note and that she wanted her brain donated to science for CTE research, and flash a gun on screen before cutting the live stream off. It would later come out that Daffney had indeed taken her own life. I watched as many people I shared the backstage area in ACW with hurt mentally, emotionally, spiritually, etc by the news of Daffney's passing. Many including myself wished there was something we could have done to prevent this but knew there was nothing we could have done to prevent this. Daffney's passing encouraged me to stay in control of my mental health as just two months after Daffney's passing I would relapse in my journey with recovery from self harm. Not wanting to fall victim to defeat from my issues with self harm, remembering how much Daffney's passing effected those that loved and cared for her encouraged me to get my life back on track. If you or someone you know and love is struggling with mental illness, I pray for and encourage you to seek help.

Shannon "Daffney" Spurill's wish was to bring awareness to the issue of Chronic Traumatic Encephalopathy aka CTE. So in loving memory of Daffney and to pay respect to what she did within the industry of Professional Wrestling let me educate you a bit on just what CTE is and who it effects. CTE is a progressive brain disease that can develop after multiple or repeated head injuries such as concussions and blows to the head. It's caused by a build up of tau protein in the brain, which can lead to nerve cell death and brain damage similar to that of Alzheimer disease. CTE can effects athletes, military personnel, and others who participate in activities that involve head impact. CTE can only be diagnosed after a person's death during an autopsy of their brain.

I remember not long into my time with ACW, heck might have even been when I was still paying my dues as In Ring Security, a female wrestler by the name of Missy Sampson had announced her retirement. Similar to a Ten Bell Salute when a wrestler or someone highly respected in the industry passes away, when a wrestler announces their retirement at a show in the ring, it's only respectful for the entire locker room to also gather around the ring in support for that person as it's not easy to walk away from something you love like professional wrestling. Think of something you personally have poured your heart and soul, blood, sweat, and tears, LITERALLY, into and now it's time for you to say goodbye to that thing. It's going to be hard as heck for you to walk away. Your probably gonna shed even more tears making the freaking announcement. And someone like Missy Sampson who was highly respected within the independent circuit definitely wasn't an easy task for her.

    Another retirement, or duel retirement I should say that I definitely remember was during my time as an official contracted referee with ACW was when another female wrestler by the name of Tess Valentine had announced her retirement from the ring. Then in the same segment of the show fellow referee Zack Carlucci announced his retirement from the ring. Now when anyone retires from the ring, it's just common sense and respectful to go in to the ring and give that person a hug or at least a hand shake and wish them well. Especially if it's someone your close to or have a lot of respect for. Tess Valentine was someone I definitely had much respect for as I remember for the longest time wishing ACW had a women's title so when they did introduce a women's title Tess Valentine was a perfect candidate. If memory serves me correctly in the history of Rough Women Warriors and the Rouge Women's Championship, Tess Valentine was a four time Rouge Women's Champion, Heck if memory REALLY serves me correctly she was the ONLY multiple time Rouge Women's Champion in the history of RWW.

    As far as fellow referee Zack Carlucci, There 's no

doubt the level of respect I had and still do have for this man. When I doubted myself as a referee and was riddled with anxiety looking like I had absolutely no clue what I was doing in the ring, It was Zack Carlucci who told me, "I see a lot of potential in you!" I'm glad he did because at the time I most certainly did not. So when Zack retired I definitely gave him a hug and hand shake. The thing about Zack is he will retire and retire and retire but every time he retires it's not for long. That man just can't stay away from professional wrestling and refereeing especially when it comes to the Susquehanna Wrestling Organization aka SWO.

Not all my memories during my time as a professional wrestling Referee are positive though. I remember at one show I already didn't think very highly of Bones to being with. He'd always show up late to training with some excuse of, "Oh I had a appointment at the tattoo shop run late" or whatever as he was a tattoo artist outside of wrestling. He never want to stay and help tear down or pack the uHaul the Friday before a show because he, "Has far to drive to get home." And he was just the most egotistical person in the locker room even though he spent most his time in the backstage checking out the female talent so he could hit on them after the show and stalk them on social media later on. And you can't forget the face his face paint was a complete rip off of Brandon Lee's character from the action and fantasy movie "The Crow." And if that isn't bad enough Bones entire move set was nothing but moves he stole from wrestlers on TV, He had not one move that a wrestler on TV didn't do.

But sadly, all that isn't even the issue I have with Bones. The issue I have with Bones is that at one show he had the balls to walk up to me and say, "I hope you're not refereeing my match tonight. I don't want you refereeing my matches because you suck!" I was thinking to myself, "I SUCK! Bro, You're literally a copy and paste version of every wrestler in the WWE. Further more you wrestle in jeans and a t-shirt, I'm a referee and I got more gear then you!"

Though clearly as the bigger man I said, "OK" but if memory serves me correct, The joke was on him cause I WAS assigned his match that night. I was the new referee I had absolutely no room to assign myself matches and I most certainly wasn't going to refuse to be assigned a match because I respected Larry Peace and Zack Carlucci's seniority over me and their mentoring me. I was only ever give a match or two ever for a show. We usually ran six to eight matches on a show card and I was given one or two. If it was just me and Zack or Larry I might have been given a third match. Their MIGHT have been ONE time that Larry trusted me with four matches but honestly that was a lot.

Another, I wouldn't say negative memory I have but I wouldn't necessarily call it a positive memory either was regarding former TNA and NXT Superstar "The Cowboy" James Storm. Tate told us that if we had any ideas for featured superstars to be part of the ACW shows to let him know. I pitched quite a few names his way during my time with ACW but most times he would inform me, "That persons retired from the ring." One name I pitched to him was "The Cowboy" James Storm. I believe it was February of 2020 Tate had came up to me before the show and said, "Good News brother, I got James Storm for a future show." I was so excited, I had hyped up James Storm to Tate with all I had in hopes he would look into booking him.

Now I only ever heard positive things about James Storm when it came to the industry but what I'm about to tell you changed my outlook on him completely and made me lose all respect for him. When Tate told me he got James Storm for a future show, he told it to me like it was a done deal. Closer to the time of the ACW show that James Storm was booked for and that we had advertised him for, James began to change his price for his appearance on the show. Tate eventually had enough of James changing the price and just threw out the idea of James being part of the show. So instead he went with his always trusty, never failed, one call away, The Sandman to appear at that up coming ACW show. I felt like a complete idiot because I had hyped up James Storm so much and put in such a good word for him to Tate and the fact Tate actually took my suggestion into more then just consideration shocked the absolute crap out of me.

So what James Storm, pretty much stiffed Tate and ACW by raising his price to appear over and over again after Tate and him already had an agreement made me look bad. I don't think I ever suggested any one else to appear at ACW after that. So yeah, I guess it's safe to say since that day I got beef with James Storm. I feel like an apology is definitely due but him being a big name and me being a no name means he does not give a rip how I feel. I still respect James Storm for his in ring career as one of the greatest tag team competitors of all time, but personally I can't match that same respect for him outside the ring or when it comes to managing his bookings. Call me crazy, But I feel like as a man your word is your bond, If you don't have your word to stand on, what do you have to stand on exactly!

Lets end on a good note here as far as memories from my time as a referee of professional wrestling. Actually if you want to get technical this memory comes from my time doing In Ring Security. I was working a show that Steve Corino's son Colby Corino was also working and when he came to the ring he took his tank top off. As part of my job to retrieve any clothing, accessories, titles, etc from the ring after entrances to took Colby's tank top and held onto it until the end of the match. After the match Colby had left the ring on the far side from where I was stationed. During intermission I headed backstage where I first encountered LuFisto and I asked her, "Where's Colby?"

I went on to tell her that, "He left his shirt" as I held his shirt in my hand. LuFisto informed me that he was probably further backstage, So I ventured further backstage. Eventually someone, I forget exactly who had informed me that Colby had left after his match. Knowing I could probably get a hold of Colby via a message on social media I took his shirt home with me. I messaged him on social media telling him he left his shirt at the venue and that I had it. I went on to tell him that if he could let me know the next time he'd be at an ACW show I'd bring it to return it to him or that if he could give me an address I would also mail it to him.

    I described the shirt to him as well as a white tank top with red tie dye spots and the words, "Kawaii AF" on it. Colby messaged me back thanking me and told me that I could just keep the shirt and that it was actually one of his favorite shirts. Part of me felt bad, but another part of me was like, "Oh my god, The son of ECW legend Steve Corino just told you that you can keep a shirt, THAT HE WORE!" Truth be told I never did wash that shirt and to this day still have it hung up in my mancave/office area of my house. Is that weird, probably, but guess what I don't care. Now Colby works in NWA where he's absolutely killing it, So I can say, "I have a wore shirt by NWA superstar Colby Corino!"

June 22nd, 2019 at a privet show ACW was asked to do was the first time I'd step into a wrestling ring as a Professional Wrestling Referee.

The Stevens Fire Company in Stevens, PA was the home of most of the Atomic Championship Wrestling shows during my time with ACW.

## REF AXL FOX

Scotty Jefferies teaching me the hard way that if you're going to be part of the show you don't heckle the talent.

The Reverb Nightclub in Reading, PA was where I got to make my debut as a Referee with Atomic Championship Wrestling.

## JAIME MOYER

*Photo Credit: DragonWolf Photography*
I had the honor of refereeing the 2nd only Texas Bullrope Match in Atomic Championship Wrestling history at a show in 2019.

*Photo Credit: DragonWolf Photography*
Scotty Jefferies vs Bones in a Texas Bullrope Match

# REF AXL FOX

*Photo Credit: DragonWolf Photography*
Twisted Tate was the man who took a chance on me when no one else would.

*Photo Credit: DragonWolf Photography*
Taking a ref bump was something that was on my bingo card since day one. Scotty Jefferies helped me to be able to cross that off my list.

111

# JAIME MOYER

*Photo Credit: DragonWolf Photography*
Scotty Jefferies was someone I always felt safe in the ring with. And if there was anyone I trusted to take a bump from it was him.

Former ECW Superstar The Sandman was someone I always enjoyed seeing at shows. If you're wondering yes he can put away a beer in person just as well as he can on TV.

## *REF AXL FOX*

James Ellsworth is the perfect example of don't judge a book by it's cover. This "no chinned doofus" turned out to be one of the most genuine people I've ever met in this industry.

November of 2023 I made the toughest decision of my career and that was to hang up the "zebra stripes" and retire from Refereeing.

*JAIME MOYER*

## Chapter XII

## Going Off Script

"Off Script" is a term in wrestling used to describe when a wrestler cuts a promo be it in the ring or out of the ring and they say something that wasn't part of the plan for them to say during said promo. Usually going off script leads to a wrestler getting in a lot of hot water. I bring this up because that is what I'm about to do in this chapter. I'm going to be talking about some issues I see with the independent wrestling scene not just in Atomic Championship Wrestling and Rouge Women Warriors but in the entire independent wrestling circuit. This chapter very well could get me Blacklisted within the wrestling industry, which basically means no promotion wants to work with you. Since I'm retired from the ring now I really don't care if I'm Blacklisted or not so buckle up and lets go for a bit of a ride shall we.

## *JAIME MOYER*

First lets start off with a topic I really don't care about but I was forced into caring about when I was signed with Atomic Championship Wrestling and Rouge Women Warriors. Alongside being owner of ACW and RWW, as well as a wrestler known as Twisted Tate, Tate handled the promotion of ACW and RWW shows. It's the job of the promoter to obviously promote the show so that as many people know about the show come showtime as possible. A major tool in promoting anything is the world wide web and social media. In 2016 I made the decision to delete my Facebook and Twitter and only use Instagram for social media. Tate told me, "You need to have Facebook because it will help promote the shows more."

Now my issue with that is that one, I was a referee, nobody cared what I said or thought as long as I gave the win to their favorite wrestler, and two, Wrestlers don't even promote shows unless it's their match and it benefits them. As a referee it wasn't my job to promote the show but yes I saw Tates point in that by me sharing the posts about shows people I'm friends with online that Tate may not be or that don't follow ACW online will see about our upcoming show. So for this reason I caved to my personal feelings about Facebook and made a new Facebook account. I decided that I'd only allow fellow wrestlers, mangers, show personnel, etc to follow and be my friend on my Facebook with the exception of a select few die hard fans of ACW and RWW. I think if memory serves me correctly I did later end up making a fan page for other fans of ACW and RWW to follow me on. Those pages have since been deleted by my own doing.

Sticking with a topic regarding social media but also regards fans of professional wrestling that I have an issue with. Fans who think it's acceptable just because you can go online to places like Wikipedia or whatever and find out a wrestlers birth given name or because they hear a wrestlers real name being said on the show that it's alright for them to address that wrestler by their real name. For example when Roman Reigns revealed he battles with leukemia and he started his promo out by telling everyone his name is Joe. That is not in my opinion him giving you the permission or right to when you see him be it at a show or in public call him anything other then Roman or Roman Reigns. Respect goes a long way and to address a wrestler by anything other than their wrestling name, unless given direct permission from that wrestler, is highly disrespectful in my opinion. It's like when your in school sure you might know the teachers first name because you saw it on the school website or whatever but you addressing them by anything other than, Mr, Mrs, Miss, Ms, insert last name, is disrespectful unless they tell you you may call them by something else.

I've yelled at my own mother after a show for sitting in the audience during a show and yelling, "Lets go Jaime" or "Go Jaime!" I've had to tell her on numerous occasions that my name once I get to that venue especially in the vicinity of the fans is Ref Axl Fox, Referee Axl Fox, Axl Fox, or Axl. This is not only a respect issue but also a personal security issue. Revealing a wrestlers birth given name is not only disrespectful but it puts their life outside the ring in jeopardy. People do stalk and harass wrestlers in public. By revealing a wrestlers birth given name you could be opening the door for someone less trustworthy nearby to try and use that to find out even more personal information such as were a wrestler lives or where they are staying, etc.

An issue I have with the professional wrestling industry as a whole not just within the independent circuit and this the major leagues try their best to keep under control but an incident does occur every now and then is disrespectful fans. Now when I say, disrespectful fans, I'm not talking fans who boo the good guy or cheer the bad guy, or the fans who yelled, "You suck" during matches I refereed. I'm talking about fans who think they can do or say whatever they want and get away with it just because they paid for a ticket to the show with their money. I'm talking about fans who take it to the extreme, for example when I female wrestler comes out and decides to hug a random fan and that fan decides to cop a quick feel and grab her butt. Or fans who when there are females in the ring decided it's appropriate to yell out things like, "TAKE YOUR TOP OFF!" Like seriously, We get it, You're obviously drunk and have no respect for another mans daughter, sister, wife, fiance, girlfriend, etc.

I've always been a man who has prided himself on respecting women. If I see a man disrespecting a woman in public as long as I feel safe inserting myself into the situation in defense of the woman I will get involved.

## REF AXL FOX

Women have fought hard for their respect in this business. At one time women in the big leagues, especially in WWE were highly sexualized and viewed as nothing more then eye candy and an easy ratings booster. They were given matches that would only last about three minutes at best and these matches would often involve them wrestling in evening gowns, lingerie, or wrestling in a kiddie pool filled with some type of food like pudding, chocolate syrup, or whipped cream. Women like Trish Stratus, Lita, Mickie James, Victoria, Stacy Keibler, etc where all pioneers during this time in professional wrestling.

I'm not saying these women are not complete icons and legends when it comes to people who paved the way for women in professional wrestling today. But it was truly people like Charlotte Flair, Sasha Banks, Becky Lynch, and Bayley aka "The Four Horsewomen" of professional wrestling along with Nikki and Brie Bella, Alica Fox, Tamina Snuka, and Naomi in 2015 who would take women's wrestling from basically soft core porn and elevate it to a level where women were actually competing in the main event in ten to fifteen minute matches if not longer. This time in women's wrestling would be dubbed the "Women's Revolution" and is truly one of the greatest moments in professional wrestling history. In my opinion it was Charlotte Flair vs Sasha Banks vs Becky Lynch in a Triple Threat Match at Wrestlemania 32 for the WWE Women's Championship in 2016 at AT&T Stadium in Dallas Texas that really put elevated women's wrestling to new heights. This match proved that women were deserving of more TV time and did indeed deserve to be treated with the same respect as their male counter parts. This is why even on the independent circuit women should be respected by not only the promotion they are working for but the fans as well.

An issue I have with most major league promotions, and again WWE is really bad for this, is that when a wrestler from the indies is given the opportunity to come to the big leagues and sign with a company like WWE, TNA, NJPW, AEW, etc. They are not taken seriously and are not used to their full potential. I'm talking about people like Piper Niven, Gigi Dolin, Blair Davenport, Shotzi in WWE, Britt Baker D.M.D, and Danhausen in AEW just to name a few all in my opinion are way better then they are given credit for in the major leagues. And it's not just independent wrestlers they do this with it does happen occasionally with wrestlers that come to a promotion from another promotion. Wrestlers like, Matt Taven, Mike Bennett, Jay Lethal, Juice Robinson, and Adam Cole in AEW, Bronson Reed, AJ Styles, Karl Anderson, Luke Gallows, and Xavier Woods to name a few in WWE are definitely a lot better then they are given credit for in their current promotions. Just look up The Bullet Club in any search engine and you'll see just how good Karl Anderson, Luke Gallows and AJ Styles are, Look into the history of Ring Of Honor in Philadelphia, PA and you'll see how good Adam Cole, Jay Lethal, Matt Taven, and Mike Bennett are.

Now lets move on to the biggest issue I have with

the professional wrestling industry and had lots of issues with this on the independent circuit during my time with ACW and RWW. And that's with being a Christian within an industry that prides itself on promoting conflicting values and beliefs then that of the Christian religion. I get everyone has the right to Freedom Of Religion but Christian has absolutely no place in the professional wrestling industry or at least that's the impression I got from my experience in the industry. I honestly don't know how guys like Mark Calloway aka The Undertaker and Shawn Micheals survived being in the industry being Christian men who hold their faith near and dear to them. I also understand that everyone is entitled to their own opinion but the thing about opinions are "opinions are like butt holes, everyone's got one one, and some of them stink!" I understand as well that respect is a two way street, It's earned not given.

  That being said, I had a lot of issues voicing my opinion backed by my values and beliefs from being a Christian on the topic of LGBTQ+. It seemed like people within the locker room or business could post their opinions supporting LGBTQ+, but the minute I posted my opinion not supporting it someone would run to Tate and tell him and he would make me apologize and tell me, "Stuff like that will get you blacklisted in this industry, and you don't want to be blacklisted." I'm not going to name any names as to people I had issues with concerning this and I'd be lying if I said talking with some of these people didn't help me view the LGBTQ+ Community with a little more respect then I once did. I use to be that guy that was like, "Oh heck nah, The bible says you're going to hell, and you're gonna burn nicely in hell my friend!" After talking to some of these people especially one person who I had issues with more then once I began to be more like, "Sure I don't agree with your lifestyle, But It's not my place to judge you either, So lets just agree to disagree here." I quickly found out through these issues and was even told a few times that "You're a Referee, They're Wrestlers, They're more valuable to the show then you so you need to respect them." The fact I was just a referee meant that my values and beliefs meant nothing in the situations and that the other persons values and beliefs needed to be respected.

    My faith is not up for debate, I believe what I believe because it's what I was brought up in. From a young age church and Christianity were made and important foundation for my life. As I grew older and broke away from relying on my parents I decided to continue my faith in Christ and having the values and beliefs of Christianity be a foundation for my life. To be told these values and beliefs are not important and hold less value then those of conflicting lifestyles is disrespectful to me and just goes to show how little I was actually valued when it came to being part of the roster of Atomic Championship Wrestling and Rouge Women Warriors. This was honestly another reason why retiring from professional wrestling was so easy for me and seemed like the right thing to do. I don't want to be part of an industry that won't respect my morals and beliefs, And tries to force me to respect others morals and beliefs.

## CHAPTER XIII

## LIFE AFTER RETIREMENT

I posted my retirement on Instagram on November 4th, 2023. I began training with Tate to be a referee, if I remember correctly, in the middle of November 2018. So my announcement of my retirement had come just shy of the five year mark since I began my training. Not gonna lie now that I officially was out of the industry, as an active part of it anyway, I felt a sense of freedom now. I knew that nobody could reprimand me for what I posted or said online. Not that I planned on pissing anyone off exactly either.

My mom was a big fan of Scotty Jefferies in ACW and of course Scotty was someone that I had mad respect for during my time in the industry. Scotty at this point was working for a promotion out of York, Pennsylvania known as Pennsylvania Prime Championship Wrestling or

PPCW for short. My mom told me that Scotty was going to be in a Battle Royal and that former WWE Superstar Fandango was going to be there as well. I was excited to go because I knew that since I was officially no longer tied to a promotion and that I would be attending strictly as a fan of professional wrestling who supported independent wrestling I could act a fool and get away with it so to say. Of course like old times, my mom and I sat front row and I made sure to get my picture taken with Fandango even though to be honest I thought his gimmick in WWE was quite stupid and annoying. Fandango in WWE might have been stupid and annoying but the man behind the Fandango gimmick was a pretty chill guy.

When we went to one the PPCW show they were handing out fliers promoting an upcoming wrestling show where multiple promotions within the area as well as a new promotion by the name of Three Legacies Wrestling in Lancaster, Pennsylvania were all coming together to put on one big super mega show at the Lancaster Barnstormers stadium. Three Legacies Wrestling or 3LW for short was a promotion owned by former WWE manager Ricardo Rodriguez. The bonus to this show was that aside from buying your ticket to the show you could also buy a ticket for a meet and greet with either Rob Van Dam, Alberto Del Rio, and there was another name that I can't for the life of me remember who it was. My mom and I decided to meet Rob Van Dam, which I'm glad we did because Alberto Del Rio ended up running late, which I've heard he is pretty known for, and the other person we just didn't really think they were as big as RVD and we could only afford to buy tickets to see one of the three. Security was pumping people through the meet and greets quickly as their was a lot of people to get through before the show. Rob Van Dam was such a cool guy when I got to meet him, I of course got his autograph as well as my picture taken with him.

    When It came time for the show to start it turned out to be a great show. This show was the first time I encountered a fan bothered by my heckling of the wrestlers. This was 2023 and I had been attending these independent circuit wrestling shows as a fan since 2015 up until 2018 when I decided to get into the business and I even attended shows as a fan during my time in the business as I was a true believer in the #SupportIndependentWrestling movement. So about eight years I had been attending independent wrestling shows be it as a fan or a worker. I forget exactly what I yelled out, I think it was a gay joke or something like that and this guy sitting behind me taps me on the shoulder. Beings it's a baseball stadium and seating in stadiums does tend to be tight I ignored it taking it as someone probably just bumped my shoulder on their way out of the row behind me.

    Again, the guy taps me on the shoulder only this time I turned around expecting someone to be like, "Oh, I'm sorry" because their knee kept bumping me or something but now it was this guy who informed me that he is gay and that my, ""homophobic slurs", are not necessary."" I forget exactly what I said in reply but it was something along the lines of telling him to, Shut up and that this is America and under the First Amendment I have the right to Freedom Of Speech. I turned back around to continue watching the show and the guy and what I can only assume was his boyfriend got up and left. Now looking back on the moment my actions where anything but Christian or acceptable. But the Anarchist in me took over in that moment.

When it came time for Rob Van Dam to have his match I was super excited as Rob Van Dam was someone I was a huge fan of being a fan who's passionate about hardcore wrestling and Rob Van Dam being a former ECW Superstar. Rob began his match and he just looked super sloppy in the ring, he could barely even run right. I leaned over to my mom and said, "Holy S**t, He must be high out of him mind!" I knew Rob Van Dam was a stoner as I'm sure most people know because he doesn't exactly hide it. But my god, This was bad, I never witnessed anyone in a wrestling ring who was so baked they could barely function. I've known people who smoked backstage before the show, I won't name any names, but again Rob was on a whole other level of baked, cloud nine thousand nine hundred and ninety nine for sure.

PPCW would eventually relocate to another venue in the York County area and of course my mom and I went because again Scotty Jefferies was on the card. Shortly before the date of this particular show by step brother had a falling out at my grandparents house with my uncle and my grandparents that resulted in the cops being called and my grandparents making the tough decision that my step brothers mental health was to much for them to handle anymore and that he needed to move elsewhere. My step brother can't live on his own as he suffers from Cerebral Palsy as well as the progressive stages of Multiple Sclerosis. In fact his whole issue with his mental health was that being caused by his Multiple Sclerosis he was experiencing auditory hallucinations. He had originally called me to see if I would take him in but beings I live in a two story apartment on the second and third floor with at least fifteen steps just to get to my front door it wouldn't be a good idea due to his condition making stair climbing a struggle. So my mom ended up taking him in.

    My mom lives with her second husband who also is a wrestling fan so WWE RAW and WWE SmackDown are weekly viewed in their house. My step brother began to watch WWE which was completely news to me. He came with us to the upcoming PPCW show but for this show we got general admission tickets instead of front row. I joked with him asking him who his favorite wrestler was thinking he didn't even know any wrestlers aside from the big names like Stone Cold, The Undertaker, Kane, Mick Foley, etc. To my surprise he said, "I really like Shinsuke Nakamura." Of course he does, my step brother is a fan of Japanese culture thanks to his love of video games.

    My mom and I added my brother in getting up the few steps in the venue as he was to stubborn to take the entrance they had reserved for disabled people. Of course once we got settled my mom and I had to go to the merchandise area where Scotty Jefferies was set up and say hello to him and introduce him to my step brother. Once the show began it was time for some women's action. It was a match between two women on the independent circuit who aren't afraid to shed a little blood for the entertainment of the fans in attendance. One of the women was Rebecca Payne, a woman I was familiar with from attending ACW shows as a fan before my time in the business. At one point the woman who Rebecca was wrestling pulled out a butterfly knife and slit Rebecca's forehead wide open, blood flowing EVERYWHERE!

    The two women fought their way over to where my mom, my step brother and I were sitting. My mom and me moved out of the way the best we could, my step brother couldn't really move his wheelchair walker in tight spacing. Rebecca's opened looked at my step brother and said, "You okay with a little blood?" My brother said, "Yeah" and Rebecca's opponent slammed Rebecca's head onto the now empty chair beside my brother and blood went everywhere. Needless to say my step brother thought that was the coolest part of the entire show. He just couldn't stop talking about it the entire hour drive home.

    Knowing the recent stress my step brother had been through hearing how much he enjoyed the show and especially that one match was so great to hear. I felt the need to reach out to Rebacca Payne on social media and fill her in on what my step brother had been dealing with recently and inform her on how much he enjoyed her match. She replied back to me telling me that she was glad to hear my step brother enjoyed the spot in her match and that some fans weren't happy with the spot. She also informed me that she would bring a few 8x10's to the next PPCW show and sign one for my step brother. I also informed her that he was worried about her beings that she bleed so much but I told him how crazy she is and how she lives for spots like that in her career. She must have shared my message with the woman she was wrestling that night cause she told me how much my message meant to not only her but to the woman she was wrestling as well.

    We haven't gone to another independent wrestling show since that night though. I don't know why though, I guess life between my mom, my step brother, and I had just gotten busy but I'd definitely like to get back going to shows again. Especially now that there is a promotion again here in the Lancaster, Pennsylvania area. After Tate hadn't put together any ACW shows after the pandemic there really wasn't any independent wrestling promotions in the area. To go to any independent wrestling shows I'd have to travel to other counties nearby. Until, Three Legacies Wrestling came along.

    And again beings Three Legacies Wrestling is owned by a former WWE star I can definitely see becoming a regular fan of that promotion. 3LW is also a great promotion because Ricardo partners with guy who is a former drug addict so they tend to do a lot of charity work to help recovering drug addicts. And that is definitely something that I can get behind and support. Chris is the name of the guy that partners with Ricardo to manage 3LW, I believe Ricardo also has a history with recovering from drug use as well. There are a lot of wrestlers even in the big leagues who got into the industry to escape things like addiction, crime, mental health issues, etc. I actually am one of those people as I began training a month after I began to self harm as a result of my mental health getting worse and worse.

     Just three months prior to my announcement of my retirement from refereeing professional wrestling I wrote my first book, *"Fearless Over Failure"* which is essentially a memoir of the life up until the point of writing the book. I talk in that book more in depth about my issues with my mental health and how getting into refereeing actually helped me seek help for my mental health issues. That book is available through most major online retailers such as Amazon, Walmart.com, and BarnesAndNoble.com. I still watch professional wrestling on television religiously. I watch WWE, TNA, AEW, and ROH products regularly. I enjoy watching people I worked with on the indies like Lady Frost, Queen Aminata, Jordynne Grace, and others absolutely killing it in the big leagues.

     Now my main focus is on my career in Softball, playing for my churches Softball team in a church Softball league. I began playing church softball in 2013 when I was still attending the church I began attending as

## *REF AXL FOX*

a kid called, Grace Fellowship Church of Ephrata. On that team we played in the New Holland Church Softball League. I now play for Reamstown Church Of God where I played my first season with them in 2020 and am still currently a part of their team. I play the position of Catcher for the most part but occasionally get played in Right Field as well. I promise I'm much better at Softball then I was at Refereeing in Professional Wrestling and have no desire or intentions of retiring from that any time soon so long as my foot keeps from giving me any issues.

*JAIME MOYER*

## RING THE BELL

    If there is one thing I want people to take away from this book and from my career as a referee of professional wrestling it's to not give up on your dreams. Had I accepted my neurologists disapproval of me wanting to become a professional wrestler, I would have never even started looking at wrestling schools for training. Now sure, I'm not saying it was a wise idea either to go against a medical professionals advice, but if you know you can do it in a safe way then that's most important. I made sure I made my seizure disorder known right off the bat to the people I asked to train me. On the same hand, Had I taken Rob Noxious rejection to train me and accepted it as defeat I would never gotten the opportunity to experience what life is like on the side of the barricade that fans aren't allowed. With that said, the other take away from this book and my career is to not let failure or rejection be an option.

    I might have came into the professional wrestling

industry at a bad time. I'm thankful for the time I did have in the business. I was able to experience what most can only dream of. I lived a life that made me a better person today. Heck if we are being honest here, I talk about my sobriety in my first book, *"Fearless Over Failure."* What I don't mention is what influenced me to become sober other then it effecting my mental health.

On February 18th, 2022, Mark Calloway a.k.a The Undertaker would take his rightful place in the WWE Hall Of Fame. I was ready and excited to see a man I grew up watching my entire life be immortalized in the WWE with one of the greatest honors ever. What I wasn't ready for was the absolute greatest speech I've ever head in my life, and a speech that would sound like The Deadman was talking to me specifically. He began to talk about how perception is reality, and how the way people view you says a lot about who you are as a person. This made me think about how I would constantly brag so much at work about my intentions to go home and drink and get drunk that my coworkers actually believed I was this raging alcoholic. That was their god honest perception of me and by no ones fault but my own.

It was that portion of The Undertakers Hall Of Fame induction speech that sparked a fire within me that ultimately would be the fire of change. The fire I needed to become a better person not only for myself but for those around me. It was time I changed the perception that the people in my life had of me. I no longer wanted to be known as the coworker who was going to go home and spend his weekend drinking more then a fish. No longer did I want to be the coworker that when people heard I called off on a Monday, everyone assumed it was because I was drunk or hungover. So in May of 2022 I decided I was no longer going to drink as well as no longer going to chew tobacco.

From this point on it was a clean and sober life for me. A life that not only I could be proud of but that would be pleasing to the Lord as well. As of writing this book I am 2 Years Sober from Alcohol and Tobacco products. I'm happier and healthier cause of it and my mental health has even gotten significantly better because of it. Who would of thought that the words of a man that most Christian people take one look at and say, "Oh my, He needs Jesus" like The Undertaker, who little do most people know loves Jesus, would influence me to make such a major change in my life that would ultimately be for the better. I'll forever be grateful for that Hall Of Fame speech.

I guess this is where I wrap thing up, The "Go Home" portion of this book. As Jaime Moyer I have and forever will enjoy professional wrestling. But as Referee, Axl Fox I'll never forget my time on *The Other Side Of The Barricade!*

*JAIME MOYER*

*REF AXL FOX*

## ABOUT THE AUTHOR

Jaime Moyer is an ENFJ personality type to the core known best for his extreme levels of energy. Jaime enjoys being outdoors taking walks through nature and cruising around on his 50cc gas powered scooter or on one of his multiple skateboards. He love to be surrounded by family and friends whenever possible, Jaime also goes by the name Axl Fox online. Jaime's hobbies include playing video games on his PlayStation 4, Skateboarding in the streets as well as local skate parks and Drawing via a verity of different mediums such as felt tip marker, colored pencil, and acrylic paint and has even won various ribbons at the local fairs for his drawings and paintings. Jaime describes himself as loyal, hard-working and dedicated. Jaime wrote and published his first book "Fearless Over Failure" in 2023 which is available through most major online retailers such as Amazon, Walmart.com, and BarnesAndNoble.com.

*JAIME MOYER*

## ACKNOWLEDGMENTS

Thanks again to "Twisted Tate" Tate Hammer for believing in my and for taking a chance on training me when no one else would. Thank you for giving Axl Fox a place within Atomic Championship Wrestling and Rouge Women Warriors.

Thank you to the fans who motivated me to get involved in the professional wrestling industry. Thank you to the ones who cheered for me and even for the ones who booed me and poked fun at me for how bad I was.

Thank you to my Mother, Sharon Cataldi, for being my number one fan and my biggest supporter through out my journey as a referee in the professional wrestling industry.

Thank you to all the Men and Women of Atomic Championship Wrestling for sharing the locker room with me and always being so warm and welcoming each and every show.

## *JAIME MOYER*

Thank you to fellow referee's Larry Peace and Zack Carlucci for also believing in me and taking me under your wings and teaching more in depth how to be a good referee withing the business.

Thank you to Scotty Jefferies for allowing me to referee most of your matches during my time in the business and even allowing me to referee such a historical match like the second ever Bullrope Match in ACW history between you and Bones. I know my lack of knowledge as a referee left you frustrated at times and I might have been a lot to work with at times but I enjoyed every moment we had.

## AUTHORS OTHER TITLES

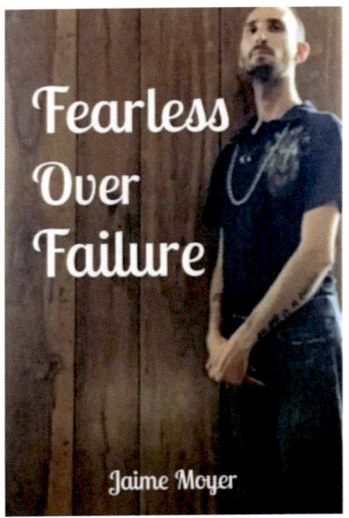

*Fearless Over Failure* is an autobiography about the life of Jaime Moyer from birth up until present day, 32 years of age.

Available: Amazon, Walmart.com, and BarnesAndNoble.com

*JAIME MOYER*

*REF AXL FOX*

*JAIME MOYER*

Milton Keynes UK
Ingram Content Group UK Ltd.
UKRC030010130724
445616UK00005B/54